To Mum and Debbie

Copyright © 2019 Robert Craggs

All rights reserved. Except as permitted under the *Australian Copyright Act 1968* (for example, a fair dealing for the purposes of study, research, criticism or review), no part of this book may be reproduced, stored in a retrieval system, communicated or transmitted in any form or by any means without prior written permission.

All inquiries to be made to the author.

National Library of Australia
Cataloguing-in-Publication entry:

Author: Craggs, Robert

Moving to Chulsa / by Robert Craggs

ISBN: 978-0-6487145-0-7

Editor: Pope, Claudette

Cover Design: Wild Weeds Press

Printer: iPrintPlus

Foreword

'Moving to Chulsa' sounded so exotic and then I discovered it was a council estate in London, not so exotic after all but it was special for Rob Craggs.

This is an emotional read; funny, sad and at times you're scared for the child growing up amidst uncertainty, people coming and going and a boy just being a boy.

However, there is a constant throughout, family. Rob's Mum and Sister and all these years later, that hasn't changed.

This story is very real, yes, 'warts and all' and other *stuff* but that's for you to find out.

There is another constant; Rob's optimism that life would get better. As he says, 'Life can be hard but children are resilient and I had plenty of spirit.' His story also reinforces the notion that pleasure can come from small, everyday things. Some of those things will surprise you!

When I finished reading the manuscript, I sent Rob an email with the comment 'Oh my, I lived a sheltered life, thank goodness!'

I also asked why his story finished when it did? I felt there was more. For him it was a fitting time to end but there is more to come and I look forward to the next instalment.

Thank you Rob for asking me to work with you to turn your manuscript into your book. It has been both a privilege and a pleasure.

Claudette

Chapters

Foreword ....
CHAPTER 1 — The Sun Does Shine........................ 1
CHAPTER 2 — As It Was and As It Is...................... 8
CHAPTER 3 — Davey 10
CHAPTER 4 — Mum's Background 13
CHAPTER 5 — Bright Lights Of London 19
CHAPTER 6 — Back Up North............................... 22
CHAPTER 7 — Fostering 28
CHAPTER 8 — Peter.. 34
CHAPTER 9 — Earls Court..................................... 38
CHAPTER 10 — Malcolm Infants School 43
CHAPTER 11 — Overcoming.................................. 48
CHAPTER 12 — Going Up 53
CHAPTER 13 — A Winner 57
CHAPTER 14 — Miss XL 60
CHAPTER 15 — As Best As Ever............................ 65
CHAPTER 16 — A Crack 68
CHAPTER 17 — Italian Blood 72
CHAPTER 18 — Assefa Berhane-Selassie 76
CHAPTER 19 — Reverse Charges.......................... 82
CHAPTER 20 — Heading North............................ 88

CHAPTER 21 — Stepping Into Agate 97
CHAPTER 22 — Bobby 101
CHAPTER 23 — Brother John 107
CHAPTER 24 — Fight 111
CHAPTER 25 — Second Biscuit 117
CHAPTER 26 — Angela and Pat 120
CHAPTER 27 — Pat and The Cop Shop 127
CHAPTER 28 — Nola 131
CHAPTER 29 — Audrey...................................... 133
CHAPTER 30 — Mums and Stereos 140
CHAPTER 31 — Kentwood Senior 149
CHAPTER 32 — Clubs, Cigarettes and Gangs 159
CHAPTER 33 — Chulsa Oak 166
CHAPTER 34 — Dare.. 171
CHAPTER 35 — Cwabby in the Cupboard 176
CHAPTER 36 — Perverts 184
CHAPTER 37 — World Cup 189
CHAPTER 38 — Windfall and Change................ 192
Acknowledgements ....

CHAPTER 1 — The Sun Does Shine

Mum says we might be moving to Chulsa. Hearing this news is like hearing a long-awaited summer has arrived. A summer without sunsets. This isn't typical news; this is an announcement of beginning, a new life; a better life and I can already feel the sun shining on my skin. I am ten, my sister Debbie is four and Mum who stands between us and the big world is thirty-one. It's spring 1969, a happy moment and a great place to begin my story.

There I was, sitting in front of the big black-and-white TV watching *Lost In Space*, on a Tuesday afternoon. Mum was in the kitchen. She poked her head around the door.

'We might be moving to a new house soon.'

This got my attention, 'Are we, where to?'

'There's a housing estate down the road, it's called Chulsa.'

'Chulsa?' 'Chulsa Estate?' I knew Chulsa, my best mates Paul Winston and Steve Hullett lived there. I couldn't wait to tell them!

For four years we'd been living up in Crystal Palace Park Road, number 69. In its Victorian hey-day, it was a mansion house complete with servant quarters, owned by a rich merchant. Like all the other detached houses on that road, all the gardens backed onto the Crystal Palace Park.

The town of Upper Norwood is by the top entrance of the park but everyone knows the area as Crystal Palace, so named after the Crystal Palace Exhibition.

The Crystal Palace, otherwise known as The Great

Exhibition, was a project of Prince Albert, Queen Victoria's husband; something to keep the young man busy while his wife ruled her empire. Built by Joseph Paxton, the palace stood at Hyde Park for a few years from 1851 until it had run its course. After that, the novelty was over. Paxton struggled to keep his creation alive and found a perfect spot to transfer it, Upper Norwood in south-east London. The structure remained there until a mysterious fire burned it down in 1936, twenty-eight years before we moved there. The ruins of that old colossal white elephant belonged to another age. And yet, here we roamed and played in its aftermath, just a handful of years later; separated from that different age where those ruins belonged, by a slim veil of time.

The ruins are still there today, a reminder of a glorious past. There are huge stone sphinx statues, magnificent rows of old stone steps, armless sculptured statues, all sandblasted and cleaned up but silent witnesses still. If you go onto Trip Advisor and type in 'Crystal Palace' there are interesting writings and comments about the area; I feel honoured to have lived there for so long. And let's not forget the Crystal Palace BBC Tower itself that towered into the sky above. People can see it from miles around as it transmits its signals for BBC television and radio for the whole of South London. Its original name was The Phoenix Tower named because the BBC built the tower on the ashes of a previous experimental structure, which burned down alongside the Palace.

By the time we moved there, all the houses backing onto the park became a shadow of their former glory. They were now in disrepair; time having swept away the former upper-middle-class life away. Private landlords now owned them and rented out a few shabby rooms on each floor to poor working-class families.

We lived on the top floor. There were two families living on each floor with a shared toilet and bathroom. Bath time in winter could not be more disagreeable, running across the cold landing on tiptoes to the cold silent bathroom. Hot water seeped out from the Ascot gas hot water system to fill the bath to about 6 inches before turning cold again. I lay in that shallow, lukewarm water as heat sucked through the cold enamel into the cool blue air; an ordeal I avoided by bathing as little as possible. I'd be shivering in that bath, too cold to get out, till my fingers looked like crinkle cut chips. By turning the tap on full for a few seconds with my toes and then turning it down to a trickle, I could get the water to come out scalding hot for all of twenty seconds. Turn it down too much and the gas would turn off, rendering the water icy cold again. After 40 minutes of fiddling, the bath was almost warm and maybe a quarter full.

Sometimes, when I didn't want to face the agony, I'd sit in the bathroom for ten minutes pretending to have a bath but Mum was onto me.

'Eh, that was quick, come here let me see', a quick inspection.

'You're not even wet, you haven't been in the bath.'

'I did but I dried myself off.'

'Well, your towel's dry and your ears are filthy, get over here to the kitchen sink.'

Soapy hot water, Mum's sharp fingernails, digging and scratching into my ears, scraping out filth.

The several families living at number 69 represented the whole of the UK - English, Irish, Scottish and Welsh. Not so many Welsh but Scots and Irish everywhere. We all got along well enough; with us children playing, fighting and arguing until the sun set, day after day after day. We'd scratch out Hopscotch grids into the hard dirt with small stones. Paul and John and I would play soccer in the park, climbing over the garden fence into the no-man's area we'd named and claimed as our own Clay Island and then over the next fence into the park. Debbie, my sister would be nearby and the Mitchells and Stewarts were always there. Sometimes David and Simon Brown from next door joined us.

In the park, we'd climb trees. It could take weeks, maybe months for us to become strong enough to climb a young oak tree and once conquered we'd hunt for the next difficult tree challenge. We play cowboys and indians and ride our imaginary horses around the garden area, improvising our story plots as the game progressed with wild suggestions.

'I get attacked by Indians and get shot by an arrow in my shoulder,'

'Yeh and I shoot him,'

'Yeh but you miss and I shoot him,'

'Yeh but you only get him in the arm and then I shoot him.'

Our main thing in common was our united dislike for our landlord next door. He was rich, we were poor, he was up, we were down, he was tall, we were short, he was straight, we were crooked, he spoke properly. But he never forgot us at Christmas. Every year he would leave a gift for us: colouring books and crayons, at each of our front doors late on Christmas Eve as if he were Santa himself. I never appreciated his kindness back then; we took our cues from our parents.

After living there a few years, Mr. Fairclough, tall, well built, with sandy grey hair and glasses, accepted an offer on his two properties, disappearing from our lives forever.

Over the next several years private investors redeveloped those houses and sold them on the private market. It was the reason we had to leave. Today they are luxury apartments. Even the basement, with the old dilapidated washroom, is now a one-bed luxury apartment.

A few weeks before we moved onto Chulsa Estate, Mum, Deb and I, walked down from Crystal Palace Park Road, a three-minute walk, to view our future home; just the three of us. Peter, Deb's dad and my stepdad was away, which I didn't mind.

Bromley Council hadn't arranged a home inspection or viewing for us. Instead, they sent a letter in the post telling Mum a flat had become available. So, we peered through the windows and the letter box. 'It's nice Mum, which bedroom are me and Deb going to have?'

Mum didn't care; one or the other. It was on the ground floor, bare, waiting for us to move in. The most amazing thing of all? We would now have a toilet/bathroom which we wouldn't have to share with anyone. It would be our own. Our own self-contained home. At last!

There was a problem though. What about Bushy our pet squirrel? I caught him one day walking home from school with my two best mates, Paul and Steve who were the reason I was so excited about moving to Chulsa. They became my friends after my school transferred me midterm up to their 3b class, just after the Easter holidays in 1968.

Most days we walked home together from school. They would part from me as we cut through Chulsa, which was where they lived and I would carry on up the road to my house.

One Autumn day as we were cutting through Chulsa we stumbled across a baby squirrel a little way off from its mother at the back of George House. We gave chase, not expecting to catch it but to my shock, I did. This was a lottery win and I wasn't letting go. I wrapped it up in my jumper and took it home and told Mum that its mother had rejected it. Mum surprised me, I thought she'd tell me off but she didn't. I think she liked my little find, so Bushy, named after its bushy tail, joined our family. Bad move? Yes; but try telling that to an 11-year-old boy!

Bushy adapted to us and was a lot of fun. We assumed him to be a boy as he often fought his reflection whenever he came near a mirror. He pooed everywhere but it was dry and if it bothered Mum, she never mentioned it. He slept in my anorak, which I hung on the living room door. He ripped out the lining in the left arm and padded out a sleeping area for himself. I'm not sure if my anorak smelled squirrel or not but I wore it to school every day after ejecting the poor creature from his home. When he wasn't asleep, he was hunting for food and he loved peanuts, which he held with his two hands to gobble down. A peanut might not sound much but imagine holding a peanut the size of a rugby ball and polishing it off in one go.

Mum sometimes had parties at our house and Tam, one of Mum's friends, often came to them until he punched Mum in the ribs and his company was no longer required. I'm sure he didn't mean it; he was usually a lot of fun to be around but he could be possessive with Mum.

Anyway, one night before things turned sour between them, Mum had a few friends over in the evening. They were drinking and carrying on and Tam was sitting in the chair by the door arguing with someone; a friendly drunken brawl. All the noise must have woken Bushy, who came out of his anorak nest to investigate. Then, with one jump he pounced and landed straight onto Tams baldhead. Everyone froze, not only by the sudden sight of Bushy sitting on Tam's head but also by Tam's alarmed expression. He didn't know what had happened. No-one knew we had a squirrel! Mum burst out laughing and then, as realisation swept around the room, each of them, one by one, erupted into thunderous roars, even Tam.

Boy, I miss Bushy. Bromley Council's firm policy, was, 'No pets' on Chulsa Estate! Humbly accepted without question. We didn't consider that Bushy wouldn't able to defend himself in the wild. We didn't think to ask any of our neighbours if they'd like a pet squirrel. So, the day before we left Crystal Palace Park Road. I took Bushy down to the garden and told him we were leaving and he couldn't come with us.

I walk toward a tree in the garden, all the time explaining to Bushy he has to go. I'm crying. When I put my cupped hands up to the trunk, I hope that he might shy away and bury himself in my shoulder. Instead, he takes off up the trunk of the tree and doesn't look back.

A few months later some of our old neighbours tell us that Bushy keeps coming back up the balcony and they often feed him but I never see him again, nor do I ever look back; Chulsa Estate is calling me and I turn away from what has been a beautiful and unusual experience.

CHAPTER 2 — As It Was and As It Is

Today, Chulsa Estate is a clean, leafy green housing estate with a 90% home ownership. All thanks to Maggie Thatcher and the Conservative Party's 'Right to Buy' policy, which welcomed the poorer working classes into the real estate club.

This started back in the mid-eighties. Working-class people living on council estates weren't upwardly mobile with professional jobs, striped ties and eggshell-veneered business cards. But they could now take charge of their destiny and achieve the new English dream of home ownership. Well, that's what we thought. Home ownership may have increased but no-one appeared to be in control of anything, let alone destiny.

My mum's one of the few people on the estate who still rents. We could have bought her flat with a 70% discount but I'm glad we didn't go ahead. I'm not keen on doing business with family despite it being a way of getting ahead.

I didn't realise it but compared to other housing estates, Chulsa was and is, a pearl. Set among oak, chestnut and holly trees, the flats are only four storeys' high, are not imposing and the grass areas have always been well-maintained.

Green shrubbery now replaces the broken bicycle sheds with the battered and paint peeled doors and the council has revamped the rotten garbage areas and modernised the flats with double-glazing, central heating and security intercom systems. The graffiti has disappeared, the lifts always work and the smell of stale urine has long gone. The block where we lived was called

Beacon House and it even had its own personal Maintenance Manager.

If I could, I would buy Mum's flat, even without the discount. Imagine a stranger living there after she dies! My mum and her flat are a link to a fantastic past. My past. When she dies, I'll no longer be able to wander in and out of my old life and I imagine I'll be without anchor.

We eventually lose our anchors in life. Our old loved homes, mates, wives, husbands, pets and health. Some husbands and wives stay together until they die. I even knew a couple who committed suicide together to avoid being left alone. But old age and death rob us of everything. Many of us become strangers in the areas we grew up in, many end up in nursing homes cared for by people we don't know. Anchors fail.

I have prepared myself; my old home will become someone else's memory.

But is there something in life we can keep?

Yes, I believe so.

CHAPTER 3 — Davey

By comparison with other families around us, we are poor, living on social security. We don't have carpets and our furniture is sparse but we like the standard mission brown floor tiles and we're unaware of any lack, to us, we now live the modern life.

Our windows had a double latch which could be locked in a semi-closed position, allowing outside air to circulate throughout the house without the fear of someone breaking into our home. We had two sheds; one out in the common landing which was our coal shed for a few days and one outside which was a storage shed and then my bike shed until it progressed to a motorbike shed. After many years, both sheds ended up storing junk: old Christmas decorations and unwanted ornaments stuffed into plastic carrier bags. It also became a temporary hiding place for one of Debbie's boyfriends. He had been sleeping in there for a few nights after she'd finished with him; the poor boy couldn't handle being away from her and fell apart. He's OK, now!

Davey Stewart helped us move into our new home with his painting and decorating lorry. It didn't take long; we didn't have much stuff, having lived in the furnished rental up the road. I think we did the whole move in one journey.

I think Davey was in love with Mum; he used to come to our flat every Thursday evening. He'd sit opposite Mum on the sofa and they'd drink cider and sherry and talk into the night. Whenever Davey got drunk, his eyes bossed outwards, with one eye looking upward at an angle, with the other one looking somewhere to the left. I never learned which eye to focus on when he was drunk. I liked him, he always spoke in a kind voice and he was genuine. He'd pull me over after he'd had a few and put his arm around me saying, 'Rober, yur a goo lad.' And I would smile because I believed him, every time. We were of one tribe, all of us; me, Mum, Deb and the Stewart's and it was comforting to be a part of that.

I didn't mind that Davey tried it on with Mum a few times, she wasn't interested in him anyway but had a lot of time for him. Mum always listened to him as he lamented his wife's lack of interest in him. Apparently, she, Ann, was seeing a fella at the nursing home where she worked and wasn't discreet about it. She must have lost respect for him. He had no power. Ann had it.

Whenever we had a party, which was often, we could always count on Davey singing, 'There was a soldier.' We sat around in silence listening to his grave rendition. No party was complete without this contribution from Davey. It was mesmerising. I would bury myself into a chair trying hard to make myself invisible in case Mum noticed me and sent me to bed.

Davey's grave voice brings the room to stillness. I want to be the soldier but I don't want to face the trial he faces. Ann is wiping tears from her eyes and I wonder if she still loves her Davey.

After he finishes, there're a few moments of silence out of respect before the party tries to regain itself, limping onwards but out of momentum. Within ten minutes, Davey slumps forward asleep, mouth wide open and drooling. Whenever he sang, it was his Swansong for the night.

Billy Connolly once joked that Scottish people often sing songs about missing their Bonnie home of Scotland and there'll be tears in their eyes as they sing 'going home to

Scotland'. 'But,' Billy notes: 'They're singing that song in a Glaswegian pub.'

For many passionate Scottish people, their Scotland, the Scotland that stands alone and independent from England, is a million miles away and not a few hours away up the M1. Davey and many Scots like him, carry a romantic passion for their homeland and they're pining for a country that no longer exists. It only exists in their tales of old.

A few years after we moved onto Chulsa, Davey died. He was sitting in his chair and in a moment, he was gone, just two weeks after packing up smoking. He was forty. They played 'There Was a Soldier', at his funeral and afterward we ate egg sandwiches and drank tea at the wake in the Stewart's kitchen. Outside it was a typical midweek afternoon, as grey outside as it was in the colourless living room. I don't know if Ann carried on her love affair. I wondered whether she might marry her lover now she was free. But I don't think she did.

In my fifties, I will realise that Davey's Scottish soldier and his experience as told in the song, are synonymous with many of our lives. I will learn much from pain over the years and will earn my place in the tribe; the tribe for the broken, the hopeless, where mistakes are allowed. All we need is the want to love.

CHAPTER 4 — Mum's Background

Neither Deb nor I are aware that life is a struggle for Mum. We know nothing of the daily problems she faces in trying to bring us up. She's about thirty and going through a divorce from her husband. He's in prison. We're living on social security but she secretly has a part-time job as a cook in my Aunt Viv's and Uncle Ted's cafe.

Social Security didn't know about this little arrangement but occasionally a neighbour would tip them off and then Mum couldn't work for a while for fear of losing her payments. We didn't appreciate what the Social Security was doing for us and didn't like being watched to make sure we weren't ripping off the system.

Her work in the cafe wasn't enough to support us but it did put treats on the table. The extra money also put bottles of sherry in Mum's cupboard and packets of cigarettes in her handbag. The government created social security to help people with basic needs but not treats. We didn't understand that back then but thank goodness we had that protection; it kept us from ruin. That was England; with its incredible welfare system. But living on welfare added to our stigma; single mother, living on social security, husband in prison, two children from a marriage and a love affair, one white, the other a half-cast; goodness the seventies hadn't even arrived yet. When the seventies did show up, our suburbs were only just waking up to the sixties! We had to wait until the late eighties before our kind of family became fashionable.

Some aspects of Mum's lifestyle may have reflected what the counterculture revolutionists back in the sixties applauded. Yes, we were a multicultural family raised by a woman without the help of a man. That was pretty counterculture back then. But those cosmopolitan hippies weren't living in south-east London. Neither was Angelina Jolie.

Mum hadn't even intended to sign up for this, it was an accident, a misunderstanding. Mum was just a working-class girl from the north-east of England, a Geordie, from Birtley, a small town just south of Newcastle-Upon-Tyne. What was she even doing in London? She should have been living up north somewhere married to a miner. But she had left her little town in the north-east of England to head for London. Why did a young seventeen-year-old girl leave her Geordie home in the 1950's?

To follow her big sister, Vivian.

Vivian had been living in London for about a year. Why was Vivian living so far from home? To understand this, we have to go back to my grandparents, Robert and Eva Craggs.

Robert Craggs was a very handsome man, dark with piercing blue eyes that made him look exotic, Anglo-Indian looking. He left school at 11 years old to work on a farm that his family worked on but he hated it and ran away to join the army at 16. After lying about his age and joining up, the army sent him to India for four years. Back in those days, the British had a strong presence in India protecting British interests (not very different from the American army's presence in Iraq to protect American oil interests). In the army, he trained to be a mechanic and that became his trade for life. When he left the army, he developed a passion for motorbikes and this interest drew him into a friendship with Norman Holmes. Norman had a sister called Eva.

Eva came from a miner's family. She was the youngest, the prettiest and a little spoilt due to an accident at school that left her deaf in one ear. She'd been playing in the playground when a boy kicked a football, which hit her hard on the side of her face. The impact caused her a lot of ongoing pain and the deafness increased throughout her life despite medical treatment and many 'spiritual' treatments from a bunch of crazy aunts - there's always someone around who can contact a spiritual guide or two. It appeared the only thing left was to treat her as special and if she was spoiled, well it didn't ruin her, she never became nasty with it. She always had a soft nature; at least that's how I remember her.

After she and Bob married, Bob worked away up and down the country and Eva, after a bout of loneliness, fell into having an affair with a local chap. When this humiliating news reached Bob, he reacted not with divorce but by moving Eva out of the marital bedroom and into their daughters' bedroom and Bob didn't buy another bed, so Eva, Vivian and Vera slept together in the one bed from then on.

As Vivian grew up, life became too stifling in the Craggs' household. So, she sought escape. Liberation came when at seventeen she married the first boy who came along and she could get away to start a new life.

Vivian's new husband worked in the local mines and lived a few miles away in a street where his family and most of the neighbours were related. As his new bride, she moved into his home and soon earned the nickname 'princess,' but not out of affection and she soon found herself out of favour with the women in her new husband's family.

After becoming pregnant and having a baby whom she called Lawrence, she became miserable; bonding with her son was difficult. She spent every day at her mother's house; not so much to see her but to relieve herself of her motherly duties. Her younger sister Vera, however, loved this arrangement because it meant she got to play with her nephew. But Vivian grew despondent and her family became concerned for her health and welfare.

Her mother Eva's next-door neighbour, Hannah Savage, came up with a plan. I knew Hannah years later as an elderly lady and whenever I was visiting my grandparents for a few weeks, Hannah often asked me to go to the shops for her. I hated being sent to the shops, even for sixpence.

Hannah had tightly permed hair, which was thinning on top; I could see right through it. Her fingers were stained brown from her untipped cigarettes - Woodbines and she wore slippers with her stockings rolled right down to her ankles. She wrote shopping lists on tiny scraps of paper and she used a small pencil, so small I imagine she'd had it for years. It took great skill to write with it being so tiny.

I can't say I loved her home with brown pieces of sticky paper covered with flies, hanging from the kitchen ceiling like grotesque horror Christmas decorations. I'm glad she never offered to make me a sandwich.

One thing I looked forward to in her house was seeing her Mynah bird which I hoped would one day say something to me. It made a few sounds but they were unintelligible. Perhaps it was a Geordie Mynah bird.

Hannah had a lodger whom I never saw, he was always asleep in his bedroom or at work or at the pub. I couldn't imagine having a lodger in such a small home. The council built these terraced houses - two up and two down - just after the Second World War for the working-classes. They were functional, not spacious and not designed with entertainment in mind. The word 'lifestyle' in relation to one's home didn't exist in those days. The word 'lifestyle' didn't exist for the working classes.

I could go for a month in my house without knowing I have a 15-year-old son called Lewis Craggs. It would be easy for me to forget his existence. It wouldn't take much of cunning and stealth for him to smoke dope, get sloshed and have his girlfriend over for the night without me knowing if he wanted to.

For Hannah and her lodger, this could not be done. The living space they circled each other in would be considered intolerable by today's Western standards. If Yin and Yang lived in Hannah's house, one of them would be dead within weeks. Miss Piggy would be barbequing Kermit's legs, Jack would have thrown Jill out the window and Dr Jekyll wouldn't need injections to bring out his Mr Hyde.

So, three cheers to Hannah and her lodger. Their arrangement may have been born out of necessity but she never complained.

Hannah had a relative who lived in Tooting Bec in South London. After they exchanged a few letters, Hannah and Eva arranged for Vivian to abscond and rent a room in this family's home and look for a job in that area. They executed the plan with care; Vivian's husband wasn't to suspect a thing. She took just a few clothes; enough to get started.

The time came for Vivian to say goodbye to her mum, dad and sister, she boarded a coach and left her home, her husband and her child Lawrence behind and headed for a new life.

Vivian's husband was furious and my family could never see little Lawrence again and I believe our family name was mud for years. This was 1953 in a small miner's town; a woman had run away to London, leaving her husband and child. It was scandalous.

Apart from the scandal, Vera is thrilled to receive letters from her big sister bragging about her exciting new life and soon she finds life too small in her town. It won't be long before she'll ask to borrow five pounds from her dad. She will hop on a coach and head south to be with her big sister for a life of excitement and adventure.

CHAPTER 5 — Bright Lights Of London

Mum and Aunt Vivian are working as chambermaids in a West End hotel. In the evenings they go out to glitzy nightclubs. Their favourite is The Sixty-Six Club. Vivian has met someone there. His name is Ted. He's funny, charming and splashes money around. He's also married. He's also a small-time petty criminal.

One of Ted's unusual jobs was roughing up a well-known English TV actor. It was a win-win situation. Uncle Ted got paid good money and the TV star received a tremendous thrill being terrifyingly manhandled by Ted and his group of deadly looking thugs.

The TV star was murdered in 1983. At the hearing, it was mentioned that he solicited vagrant men for sex.

This shows us a dark side of London's bright lights. Sounds contradictory, 'The dark side of London's bright lights,' like 'The dark side of light.' Where am I going with this? My son Joel used to have a little Star Wars hologram which he bought at a garage sale.

From one side I can see Luke Skywalker. If I turn it slightly, it changes to Darth Vader. Good and evil sharing the same space at the same time

This reminded me of Mum's life in London. Fun and gaiety, lights and sparkle occupied the same space in Mum's circle as misery, depression, darkness and depravity. Depending on the angle you looked from at their life, you would see either lightness or darkness.

The Sixty-Six Club was also where my mum met my father, Assefa Berhane-Selassie. Assefa came from Ethiopia. Haile Selassie had sent him to the University of

London from Ethiopia to do an electrical engineering degree.

When he met Vera, they quickly started going out together and he became her 'Pygmalion,' except, rather than carving a woman out of stone, he set about creating his fair lady from a working-class girl and he took great pleasure in it. He took her to the theatre, foreign movies, art galleries, concerts, restaurants and political meetings. Assefa was besotted with her and wanted to impress and show her off to his friends. It worked. He swept Vera off her feet; she was living her dream.

What she enjoyed most was Assefa's devoted attention to her. Yes, the foreign movies were too foreign, the political meetings were boring and she found some of his friends awful and snobbish towards her. But she enjoyed him sharing stories of his home and background and he loved listening to her sing to him, which she did gladly. Her broad Geordie accent may not have fitted her sexy demure look but her singing voice did.

But they didn't have enough in common to ensure a lasting relationship and soon everything changed. Vera became pregnant. Assefa, being a gentleman, offered marriage but Vera would have to move to Ethiopia. Negative voices that had previously bounced off Vera, now surrounded her, whispering doubt and accusations into her thoughts. She was also sick with her pregnancy and this all culminated in her seeing Assefa in a more negative light than before.

She no longer saw an exotic cultured man of high calibre but now saw a black man and she felt shame. Unable or unwilling to explain to him the derision she was subjected to because of her relationship with him, she pushed him away.

It devastated Assefa but it was over; Vera wanted and needed to get back to her own kind of people. She needed assurance and acceptance from those whom she knew to be her own, especially as she was now pregnant and feeling vulnerable.

Assefa came to visit Vera in the hospital just after I was born. When he cast his eyes on me, he didn't believe I was his child and he accused Vera of having been with another man. My grandfather wanted to seek professional advice to prove whether Assefa was the father or not but Mum didn't want to pursue it and then Assefa left for Ethiopia. Mum never saw him again.

It was 1958, Vera had just turned 20, the fun ended and the short party had left a hell of a mess.

Vera's first problem was what to do with me. The advice was to give me up for adoption and she didn't have much family support back then. Her father found the whole episode too much and at first, he wouldn't accept this young baby as his grandchild.

But he comes home from the pub one night, picks up the toothless wonder and holds him high into the air. The little baby grins down at him and drools over his grandad's face. Grandad falls in love right then.

CHAPTER 6 — Back Up North

After a while, Mum meets someone. His name is Tom McCarthy. They marry and move back up north into a caravan. They're not happy together and split up after a short while. Its 1961 and I'm two years old. I don't remember Tom but I remember my grandparents from when I was very young.

If my grandad started off our relationship with a rejection, I never felt it. I have fond memories of Nana and Grandad.

I'm sitting on this big man's lap. He's under my command. I crawl up to his face with Mum's make-up bag in my hand. I plaster his face with lipstick, eyeshadow and foundation, though I'm not sure I know what goes where.

Grandad gave me lots of freedom but he never allowed me anywhere near his tobacco pipe. And I wanted to smoke it as he did; I loved the smell of the tobacco but he was firm about keeping me away from anything to do with smoking. But the more he forbade, the more I believed he was hiding something good from me. One day my moment came. I was in the living room and no-one was around and there on the table by Grandad's chair I could see his tobacco pipe and next to it, his dull golden box with the tobacco inside. I opened it up and sniffed. The spicy aroma was comforting. I picked up his tobacco pipe. It was cold; a sleeping dragon but it still had that nice smell which meant it would taste good too. So, I tried to smoke it. What a shock that was. It was ghastly. I never tried it again.

When I was a little older, Grandad would let me into his shed. It was a small shed in the back garden. He kept it tidy; everything in place, mower, saws up on brackets, the bench with a vice and pots of nails and screws. Everything quietly in order with a smell of wood and oil, especially when I planed the wood and thin strips curled off. Grandad showed me how to plane and how to sink nails with a hammer. I made a house. A small block of wood with a few nails driven into it. Everyone was proud of me. So, I made another one.

Maybe if Grandad had brought me up, I'd have become a carpenter or a mechanic. Who knows but what I liked most were words and I wrote my first song when I was seven—

'Hear the birds tic-toc, hear the birds sing, hear the birds whistle in the morning of spring, autumn, spring, winter or summer, please feed the birds or they'll die out of hunger.'

I could see Mum hiding a smile.

Two things I wanted to do was wear Grandad's cap and donkey jacket. I found this piece I'd written about them and I'm including it here as I wrote it:

Grandad

I'm standing in the kitchen
No-one here, just me
It seems I have the place
To myself

Peaceful quiet
Time is beating slow
The day
Has just
Begun

What will I do?
With this time and space
This opportunity
Rare?

Seek, explore
Go through some drawers
Hunt through cupboards
Forbidden

And then, I see
Hanging on the door
That leads
To the outside yard

Grandad's jacket
Silently waiting
To be worn
By someone
Like me

Dark thick duffel
Leather padded shoulders
Elbows
Toughened
For heavy work

Moving to Chulsa

I can't wait to put it on
Put on all that must be
I wish that I
Could wear it
Out to play

I sink my hands deep down
Down into the pockets
And strike
Cold
Clinking keys

Clutching them, I wonder
What locks, what closed doors
Will they open?
And where
Might they be?

And then
I notice
Hanging on the peg
Grandad's cap
I take it
In my hands

Tweed of earthy colours
Carefully woven
Reflecting all

*That's right
And good
And straight*

*It's lined with a satin
Of two-tone red and green
In the middle
The brand name
'Harrison'*

*Jealously protected
From unclean greasy hair
The covered logo's
The last
Thing to fade*

*I put it on my head
To be just like him
Then to my nose
And breath the smell
Deep in*

*To images of tools
Oil, work and trucks
Tobacco
Brylcreem
And grime*

Moving to Chulsa

I'm hushed into sedation
By a quiet trusting calm
That surrounds me
And holds me
Like a dove

Grandad's scent is on me
I'm covered and secure
And I carry him
Inside
To this day

CHAPTER 7 — Fostering

Mum and Tom have separated, so we move to Leytonstone to be with her sister Vivian. I think I'm with them and am, most of the time. But they move to many addresses in places like Scunthorpe and West London and can't always take me. We also live for a while with my grandparents and that's where I'm the happiest. I also spend time in foster and children's homes; that's not so good.

It's blurry but I remember more clearly the last foster home. I'm four years old. On my first morning, the father is there. He's standing in front of the mantelpiece; tall and thin with short back and sides. White shirt with sleeves rolled up under a burgundy red sleeveless V-necked pullover. A few cheerful and friendly words with me before the troubles begin; and every morning, salty bacon for breakfast.

Salty bacon wasn't my only problem; first, I wet the bed a lot and earned myself many smacks. Also, I was the youngest and only half-cast child of many children who lived there. Every push and shove passed down the line to the bottom of the heap which was my dwelling place.

What made it worse, I had to defend my mum often, as the mother there often made derogatory comments about her. I bragged how great she was. The backlash was how great she wasn't.

On one of my visits with Mum she took me out with Aunt Vivian to their workplace. Aunt Vivian bought me a packet of chocolate toffees. When I got back my foster parents took them from me and put them on the mantelpiece. I shouldn't eat all the sweets at once. That night, I wet the bed again. To punish me they gave my toffees to the other children and allowed them to chew in front of me. In my heart, I could see that all of them, especially the adults, had broken a universal law.

Not long after that, I woke up early one morning to discover I'd pooed my pants. This was disastrous and I expected big trouble. I needed to think quickly. The answer came to me. I'd take it downstairs and flush it down the toilet. But I had to go quietly without a sound, not wanting anyone to catch me.

As quietly as possible, I crept downstairs into the kitchen, terrified I'd be caught in a restricted zone, at the wrong time, with a handful of poo. Lightly, I tip-toed into the kitchen to the back door which led to the outside toilet. But the door wouldn't open. I looked to see why it wouldn't open and then discovered the bolt at the top. Even more scared now because of increasing obstacles, I grabbed a chair and climbed up onto the kitchen bench to reach it. Stretching as high as I could, I just about reached the bolt. But as hard as I tried, I could not budge it. I kept trying. Then I saw the solution, the kitchen bin! Relieved, I climbed down, opened the bin and dropped the poo into it. My problem solved at last, I went back upstairs to bed and fell asleep.

Later in the day, I had totally forgotten the nightmare. Until that is, I heard my name bellowed from the kitchen and then she dragged me over to the bin and there on top of the rubbish lay my poo. I hadn't covered my tracks and I had the guilty look of fear all over my face. Within seconds my foster dad took me by one arm and thrashed my backside while I tried to run away, spiralling around him in circles. I felt hated. All their pent-up frustrations were unleashed on me.

That's why it surprised me when one morning I woke up to something different; something outside my usual experience; natural; but something that needed to be a secret.

I woke up in a different bed, a camp bed. And I wasn't alone. I don't remember her name; she had ash brown hair and soft blue eyes. I liked her but had not had one good exchange with her up till now.

We had been sleeping top to bottom in the same bed. My feet were between her legs. What she did didn't seem wrong but we kept it quiet and told no-one. She pushed her undies to the side and guided my toes into somewhere soft and marshmellowy. 'Rub it.'

I pressed into her and rubbed. 'Like that?' I whispered.

'Yes.'

It felt heavenly. We now shared a secret and life was much more bearable. Later that day I made eye contact with her but we never mentioned it and we never shared a bed after that night. Nothing ever happened between us again but I distinctly remember she and I never had a nasty run-in after that morning.

Life can be hard but children are resilient and I had plenty of spirit. At playschool I tried daily to scoop the fish out of the water tank; and I knew instinctively I could get away with it. Flustered by our actions, the teacher would rush over and ask us to come away from the tank but as soon as she turned her back, we'd be back in again. Those fish moved fast though; I never caught one.

Another area where I misbehaved was with the books. I loved peeling the little white stickers off the books and putting them on my hands, pretending they were plasters. I kept that up until another teacher, someone stricter, stopped me.

'Little boy, what's your name?' She spoke with authority and had dark straight hair and wore glasses. She might be kind but I can't be sure.

'What's your name?' She's not letting go.

'Robert.'

'And what's that on your hands?'

'A plaster.'

'A plaster?'

I nodded. A few children stood around as the tension increased.

'And why, Robert, is it on your hand?'

'Because I cut my finger.' I took the sympathy route but she's not buying it.

'But that's not a plaster is it?'

I put on a sad face.

'Let me repeat myself, that's not a plaster is it?'

I shook my head.

'So, what is it?'

Silence and fear

'What is it and where did you get it?'

I pointed to a book.

'Did you take it off this book?'

Reluctantly, I nodded.

'That's naughty isn't it?'

This was bad. I was now nodding to my naughtiness.

'Children mustn't pull the stickers off these books must they?'

I shook my head to show her we were finally in agreement on this.

'What do we do to little boys who pull stickers off books?'

This stumped me; I didn't know the answer.

'Shall I show you?'

I nodded. Better to agree.

'We smack them on the back of the hand like this.' She took my hand and showed our audience and my good self what she meant. It stung but at least the smack was over.

'That's what we do, we smack them.' SLAP! Another demo, in case we didn't see it the first time.

'That's what we do, hard smack on the hand,' SLAP! She wasn't stopping and I couldn't hold the tears back any longer.

'Now then,' she said, 'I hope you won't do that again.'

I nodded my head to show her she had cured me of a terrible disease and I was now reborn; a newer and better person.

Then one day at the house, my foster parents were unusually nice to me and a lady whom I didn't recognise, was present. I didn't understand why they were being so nice but I accepted it. They also had presents for me; a toy watch. I put it on.

'What's the time?' someone asked.

'Two o'clock.'

Everyone laughed.

We're sitting on the top deck of a red London bus. It's one of those tour buses without a roof. Mum is with me and my grandparents too and it's safe. My nana notices my new watch and I tell her it's two o'clock. She smiles a genuine smile. I'm so happy I'm not going back.

CHAPTER 8 — Peter

Mum has met someone at the hotel where she works as a chambermaid. He's a porter there. He whistles and sings as he goes about his daily chores. His good humour helps her forget her miseries. They move from friendship to romance and now they plan to start a life together; a life that includes me.

Peter's commitment enabled Mum to get me out of foster care. After I left the home, we travelled up north to my grandparent's home in Birtley, Durham. Peter remained in London awhile to look for accommodation. I even attended school up there for a short period. Then Peter arrived, probably with news of accommodation in London. From our living room window, I saw him arriving, walking along Dorset Avenue. Dressed in his dark single-breasted jacket and trousers with black shoes, his mood looked as grey as the rain; no warm jacket for the cold wind.

He sat down and I tried to charm him with a big smile and a 'Hello,' But Peter wasn't in the mood and he couldn't fake it; there was no guile in Peter. My childish efforts hit a wall of indifference. Looking back, I admire his inability to show interest that wasn't there. Me? I could fake anything!

We later moved to Purley for a brief spell and once again I experienced some illicit tender comfort. This time, however, it was a passionate experience, more so than I'd experienced at the foster home where I'd been staying.

I'd woken up in a small bedroom on the bottom of a bunk bed with diarrhoea and had messed myself. The bedroom was unfamiliar but change was something I accepted. I assume we arrived early in the evening and being asleep, someone had put me to bed.

Everyone had gone out drinking, leaving Linda, the nine-year-old daughter, in charge. I'd woken to find her attending to me. The last time I'd messed myself, my foster parents had given me a spanking but this time I was in for a warm and delightful surprise.

Linda changed the sheets and then took me to the bathroom to wash me. Then she found me a top to wear, all the while chatting in a calm reassuring, matter-of-fact tone. Next thing I knew, we were snuggling in bed together, naked bodies joined, kissing, embracing. I don't think we had sex, not that night anyway but we engaged in lovemaking; and I've never forgotten the experience; a deep comforting pleasure. Anything and everything I needed was right there, with her.

When the adults arrived back from the pub, Linda got up and explained that I'd soiled my pants and that she had cleaned everything up and was in bed with me because I needed comforting. She knew how to handle adults. My mum came in to see me, happily intoxicated and without a shred of awareness of what her son had been doing. She kissed me on the lips, her nose and lips cold from the outside evening air. Then she slipped back to the lounge with the others. They were unaware of what was going on under their noses.

Linda's mother, Joy and partner Eve were a female couple and good friends of my aunt and uncle. Mum and Peter had become a part of their social scene. Even though Joy and Eve were an item, Joy made an occasional living in other ways. It was many years later I discovered this through conversations with Mum. The conversation came up because about a year after we'd lost contact with Eve and Joy I had suggested to a girl who lived next door to us, that if she showed me her willie, I'd show her mine. She looked concerned and said, 'I haven't got a willie, I've got a bottom.'

'That's all right,' I said, 'You can still show me.'

She was unsure but she pulled down her knickers and we showed each other our bits. It was over in seconds and then we carried on with playing normal games and I forgot all about it but she told her mother and her mother came knocking on our door and told my mother and my mother told Peter. Peter, in turn, had the difficult task of discussing sex with me. He explained that sex was only for adults and I'd have to wait until I was a man before I could have sex. Mum wasn't satisfied though.

She wanted to know where my sexual ideas came from. When I confessed to what had been going on between Linda and myself, Mum didn't doubt me a bit. She believed Linda's household had caused her to become more precocious than the average child. Mum thought she was too mature and had lost her innocence because of her parent's lifestyle. A few years ago, Mum also told me she saw a TV programme about prostitution and there was a profile on a lady who was running a lucrative prostitution business with S & M. Mum thinks it may have been Linda. She didn't remember the TV station or any details. If she did, I'd have gone looking for her!

Back when we knew Linda's family, they had moved to a lovely home in a small town called Whyteleafe and we used to stay there for weekends. They lived in a large purpose-built, white maisonette on a beautifully large housing estate set in a spacious green hilly area.

In the evening Mum would send me to bed with Kelly, Eve's daughter. Linda, being older, wouldn't come to bed until later. I'd do my damn best to stay awake and when she did finally come to bed, we were two naked, hot bodies in sexual play. During the day, we played normal games and sometimes we'd even quarrel too but she claimed me as her boyfriend and I felt special and honoured to have her, even though there was something about her that made me uneasy; she liked The Rolling Stones. She loved that 'bad-boy' image which was scary ground for me; I preferred The Beatles; much safer! But I put up with my fears and focused on her lovely blue eyes and her long fine blond hair. I loved her slight chubbiness. I loved her big or small. She plucked me out of a pile of shit and turned my lights on and I'm forever grateful for her having been in my life. Our quiet affair went on until I was six years old and we moved to Crystal Palace. Suddenly, she was out of my life.

I miss her. We were two innocent children surviving under misplaced adults. I know what we were doing was wrong; we opened doors of ecstasy before their due date. Not healthy for normal growth.

But we find deep affection in one another and we both need it. This is something we're not experiencing from our lost, young parents.

CHAPTER 9 — Earls Court

Before moving to Crystal Palace, we live in Earls' Court for about a year. First, in Filbeach Gardens for a few months and later in Warwick Road. My first memory at Filbeach? I am five and Mum is trying to coax me into taking a bath.

'No, I don't want one.'

Peter plays a cunning move, 'How would you like to go paddling?'

This sounds promising, I nod, 'Yes.'

It doesn't take me long to realise Peter has duped me. Apparently, being washed down in the kitchen sink is paddling.

I made friends with the boy next door, Tristan. We often watched telly and played games together. One late afternoon, after watching a cartoon about a child on a flying carpet, Tristan suggested we make our own out of newspaper. He found a tin of Fray Bentos Corned Beef in the kitchen cupboard. It had a key slotted onto the little tab on the tin to roll it back to open it. Tristan ripped it off, saying this key could make our newspaper fly like a magic carpet. It thrilled me to think we'd soon be flying around the streets of Earl's Court. But the newspaper ripped apart and I had to accept that we would not be flying off anywhere.

Tristan had a pet hamster; I thought hamsters could fly. One late afternoon I called on him but no-one was home. The front door was slightly open, so I went inside. I saw his hamster in its cage and I played with it for a while before taking it out to play. I tried to help it fly by throwing it up in the air to get it airborne. Each time it landed on the ground, it wouldn't run away and I couldn't understand why.. A lady dressed in smart clothes, presumably on her way home from work, interrupted me. I tried to explain to her that hamsters could fly. She seemed concerned but the hamster was already dead and she left us. I was disappointed that it didn't fly, sad it had died and guilty that it was probably my fault. I left it on top of a bin outside someone's house and headed home.

Tristan's family rightfully suspected me; the air seemed cooler in his home. Not long after, someone's cat went missing. A well-dressed man tried to get me to tell him where it was, he even offered me half-a-crown if I told him. He had the coin in his hand, dangling it in front of my eyes. I reached out to grab it.

'Not until you tell me where my cat is,' the man said.'

I wanted that half-a-crown but I knew nothing about his cat. It seemed I had gained a bad reputation.

Then we moved to Warwick Road; I mostly played out on the landing area. How was it I entered a neighbour's flat? Curiosity? I don't know. But I opened the front door to their flat; I'd entered Aladdin's cave. There were suitcases under the bed, bags in the cupboards, toothpaste, chocolate in tins, milk in the fridge and a huge jar filled with coins.

Mum and Peter were watching TV when I came in and offered the jar of money to them. I expected smiles of delight and pats on my back for this generous offering but instead, they greeted me with horror.

'Where did you get it?' Mum first, then Peter.

'I found it.'

'Where?'

'Outside.'

'Where outside?'

I'd shrug, 'I don't remember.'

'Yes, you do, where did you find it?'

I told them I'd found it in the outside cupboard but they didn't buy it.

I showed Peter the flat I'd burgled. He opened the door and looked inside but said nothing. God knows what he must have thought. Neither Mum nor Peter ever said anything. They were both dismayed and I wonder whether they might have regretted taking me out of the foster home. If they were thinking of putting me back; well, they never did.

I don't know how I met him but I made a new friend called James. He had red curly hair and was bigger than me and we used to play on the building sites where all the major roadworks and upgraded roads were built on the lead up to the M4. One day, I remember a man shouting at us from his window in a block of flats. 'What's he saying, James?'

'He has a machine gun and he's going to shoot your mum and dad.'

His words paralysed me with fear and that evening I broke down crying and told Mum that a man with a machine gun was coming to kill her and Peter. Mum and Peter assured me that James was lying. A few days later, James came around to see me; Peter told him to get lost and I never saw him again. Problem fixed. Peter could fix problems.

But I wanted friends. I had an imaginary horse I rode when I was at school and there was a black girl called Rosemary who liked me. She even taught me how to trip people over. I tried it on Charlie, the class toughie but he was too strong for me. He left me lying on the floor wondering what had happened. There was also a dark-skinned girl who lived a few doors away. We played together but I never saw her again after ending up on the bed together without our clothes on. How did it happen? I don't know. One minute we were playing and the next we were naked on the bed kissing, lost in each other with the taste of salty skin on our lips.

Then the doorbell is ringing. I look out the window and see Granny downstairs. We're frantically trying to get dressed, tugging clothes over hot sweaty skin and before I know it we're saying goodbye and Granny looks agitated. I never see her again.

Everyone at school was too normal, like in the 'Janet and John' books and I didn't feel I belonged. They chatted with me as they sat in a circle and shared my sweets but when they discovered that the sweets belonged to someone else, they abandoned me with shame. I'd found them on the ground and got myself a little party going. I'd called these kids over to sit in a circle with me as I handed out rewards to each of them, one at a time. It was like training pets. All was going so well until the playground teacher turned up with a wailing kid hanging off her arm, 'He's got my sweets!' Game over. All the kids with their mouths full of toffees looked on me with scorn. Well, it wouldn't have lasted long; pets rarely hang around after the treats dry up.

On one occasion, I had some change in my pocket. I stood at the gate and handed out coins to children like I was the playground philanthropist. Well, didn't that get me all kinds of instant friends who pleaded for a coin or two, only to then disappear into thin air! Once the money had disappeared, I was on my own.

Not that I was the good guy, I had serious loyalty issues. A boy who I liked took Charlie on. Charlie gave him a few quick jabs and left the kid in tears.

'Come on Rob,' he sobbed, 'let's go and play.'

But I backed away. I didn't want to play with a loser.

Then one day, I stopped going to school. It was easy. I left home each morning but I didn't go through that gate. Instead, I walked around the streets, called in on friends, got turned away from doors by startled mothers whose children were at school.

I wander around the streets. Wander into the church, play with the candles, light them, play with the cat, get scratched, drop the candle and set the curtain on fire, fire gets out of control, I quickly leave the church, get stopped by two men in black vicar's clothing, get asked if I was in the church, deny it, get asked if that's candle wax on my coat, nod and say 'yes,' get asked for my address, I give it.

The next day the same two men are sitting in my living room talking to Mum while I sit and play with my teddy bear. The next day, I'm sitting at my school desk while Mum talks to my teacher. Mum leaves, then the teacher gives me a look of disgust and calls out 'Robert Craggs, you're a very, very bad boy. I believe her. I don't belong, I have serious issues.

Looking back on those days and comparing myself then with who I am today, I am so grateful that by grace and mercy, I'm as normal as I am!.

But I hate that school; that's why I take days off. I'm so glad we move to Crystal Palace.

CHAPTER 10 — Malcolm Infants School

Mum, Peter, Deb and I have become a family and we've moved to Crystal Palace from Earls Court where we lived for our first several months together. This is the start of family life for us. Deb, just a little baby, was born while we lived at Earls Court and I, at the age of six, have only been out of foster care for one year.

I think I started at Malcolm Infants School in September 1964, I knew I was the youngest in the class or I thought I was, as all the kids were utterly disgusted that I wasn't seven yet. I told everyone who asked me how old I was, 'Six and three-quarters, nearly seven.' It rolled off my tongue like a political strapline.

I didn't like the class and didn't have friends there that I can recall. I found my way around and soon picked up a lunchtime job clearing away tables and chairs with a few other boys for the caretaker. The pay was good, four Pineapple Chunks – yellow, sugar coated pineapple flavoured square pieces of candy. Yum! But the schoolwork was difficult for me and I didn't like my teacher, Mrs Marsh. Well, more to the point, she didn't like me. She was plump and round and her name made me think of marshmallows but she wasn't soft. It wasn't long before I developed a very healthy respect for her.

But it all went very fast and before I knew it, I was in junior school. Due to my struggles, I was put into the 'C' stream. There was even a 'D' stream but the children there had more than learning problems, they had major issues when they had to deal with just about anything. It looked like a hard place to thrive and survive and I was glad not to be there. I liked my class and despite having another teacher who put the fear of God into me, I did settle in and began to have mates. My first best mate was Steve Webber. He was quite a little titch with deep reddish-brown hair and big brown eyes; very cute looking and very cheeky and quite dominant for a little guy. I had taken to walking to school as it meant I got to save the tuppence bus fare. On a wise day, I'd spend that tuppence on sweets and maybe, if I decided to walk home, I'd have fourpence for sweets. On a less than wise day, I'd spend my whole fourpence bus fare on the way to school and by mid-morning I didn't have any sweets left and the gloomy knowledge I was walking home after school without any sweets in my pocket. Also, on less than wise days, I'd share a sweet or two with Steve but after a little while he came to expect his morning treat, not as a treat but as his right. One day, I decided to keep the tuppence until the end of the day. 'Where's my sweets?' He looked pretty pissed off when I lied and said I'd caught the bus to school but I'd broken the spell. After that, I bought my sweets at the end of the day when I was walking home.

I've never really thought much about Steve over the years but he really was my first really good buddy. We had a lot of fun together. Sometimes, I would call for him on the way to school. I'd sit in the kitchen, where his mum and big sisters would be sitting around in their dressing gowns, drinking tea and smoking cigarettes, the smoke mixing with the hot steamy air while it rained outside. It seemed a harsh place, lots of hard words and shouting and Steve, the youngest, was the only boy. No wonder he was such a little toughie and full of cheek. Then we'd head to school, hanging out for the first play break when we could run into the concrete playground and let off some steam.

Sometimes we'd kick a ball around if we had one or we'd play British bulldog or feet off ground. Sometimes we'd just hang around in a circle and joke about, maybe show off our new Wayfarer shoes. They were the first type of brand shoes I'd ever wanted, made by Tuff. On the sole were imprints of an animal's paws, rabbit, dog, cat, fox, beaver, etc. and in the heel of the shoe, lying under a flap was a compass, so we'd never get lost and would always be able to track animals. David Gould, blessed with incredible self-esteem, (he grew up to become a car dealer) was the only one whose Wayfarer's were slip-ons. I didn't like them as they looked odd. We all stood there looking at them, asking him how come his were slip-ons and not tie-up's like ours and then Smithy went and cried out, eureka style, 'I know, you had them specially made!'

What a dunce, what a thing to say but everyone just stood there gasping and David gave that sort of smile that said, 'Yeah, you got me, how did you guess but don't spread it around.'

Stupid Smithy, then shouted out, 'I knew it, I knew you had them made!' Screw Smithy, he took the guy with the highest self-esteem and made certain he'd remain on that mountain peak for fucking ever. But ain't that life ay?

The most agile among us was Steve Dunton. With his short, straight cropped blonde hair, cheeky blue eyes and light freckles on a very pale white face, he was by far the funniest person I had ever known. Just watching him throw a stone could leave me in fits of laughter. Like Steve Webber, he was another one who was the youngest male among a throng of older sisters and he got away with a lot; so again, a spoilt and very cheeky child who knew nothing about boundaries or consequences.

I'm sorry to say as a teen he went astray and it wasn't a phase he simply went through. Not that I was innocent. In our early teens, we all stole things, usually sweets from the sweetshops. We also stole bright coloured towelling socks, which looked good with our loafer shoes. I even tried burglary with them once in my mid-teens but I didn't like it, it was too scary, so I backed away. But I think Steve carried on and as an adult, he spent some time in prison; then he hit alcohol and his life was ruined. I bumped into him once in my forties and the poor fella was a shadow of his former self. Consequences had finally caught up with him. It was sad to see him like that. Who would have thought that such a sad future was in store for him? I believe he died in his mid-fifties of alcohol-related problems.

It was Steve's pushy and adventurous nature that made him the first to be able to leap from the playground wall onto the metal horizontal bar and it was weeks before we could do it. It was scary because in order to jump from the wall and catch hold of the bar meant using faith and leaping out almost horizontally. It was the same sort of stance you use when diving into a swimming pool but we were diving out over hard bitumen and if we missed, it wouldn't be pretty. There was that frightening moment of being out there in the air with no going back and having to catch the bar or suffer the consequences. It took time and a lot of half-hearted attempts until slowly one by one, we all managed to do it and it felt exhilarating! I think it was my first experience of extreme danger sport and it was Steve who pushed us to our limits.

There was a time though when it didn't work out too well for him. One morning during assembly the headmaster, Mr Jennings addressed us all about a break-in at the school. This concerned me for a moment because about a week earlier a handful of us had gotten together after school, broke into the shed and got all the rubber bouncy inflatables out and were bouncing around the playground on them.

Thankfully though it wasn't about that.

Someone had broken into the actual school building through the skylight. It was then, sitting as we were, cross-legged on the ground being addressed by Jennings that I noticed Steve. He had cuts all over his face and was black and blue all over. He really didn't look too good and he walked with a limp. Goodness knows why he came to school looking like that. And yes, it was rumoured that he had broken into the school and whilst standing on the skylight trying to open it, the bloody thing gave way and he went crashing through it.

Fifty years have gone by and I managed to catch up with Ray Spearman. I shared this story with him about Steve breaking into the school and falling through the skylight. It turns out that Ray was holding Steve by his wrists, pulling him up through the skylight, when he decided it would be fun to let go of Steve. This sort of prank was very common amongst all of us.

CHAPTER 11 — Overcoming

I'm enjoying my new life, though I'm not particularly fond of the two brothers next door, Simon and David Brown. Even though we play together, they're often cruel, calling me a dunce and scruffy. Simon and I are the same age, seven years old but he's stronger and tougher and he often reminds me of that fact and boy can he throw a punch! He has brown hair, blue eyes and a small mouth with thin lips, which make him look intense and angry. I think he lets out his angry frustration when he belts me because his big brother often beats him. His brother David is a year older than us and blessed with light, easy hair and good-looking carefree features. He never becomes physical with me; he simply dismisses me as a lower being in his kingdom.

They were smart boys and came from what I imagined to be the quintessential white, middle-class family. TV taught me their example set the moral benchmark because they were good people. But their goodness didn't flow towards me in any kindness, so I assumed I must be bad.

Paul Fisher was more civil. He lived next door to the Stewarts' on the floor below us. He was an only child and his parents looked older than the norm. They weren't friendly but polite and reserved. I think they were middle class and their son attended the prestigious Dulwich College. It seemed odd that the Fishers and the Browns lived in rented accommodation as they didn't appear to be poor. Both families carried an air of snobbery. Everyone else was either Irish, Scottish or people like us.

Even though Paul was much nicer than David and Simon, he and I still clashed, which often left me with a black eye or a bleeding nose. As long as I played by his rules, life was OK and anyway, he had a good influence on me; he was a good boy, not a trouble seeker.

Paul had good games; Cluedo; a 'whodunnit' detective board game and Subbuteo, a soccer game played on a rolled-out piece of felt. He also had Monopoly and many other games. We played well together, especially as I accepted he knew practically everything and I knew very little. I questioned him, 'Do you know everything, Paul?'

He thought for a moment and then replied, 'No, not everything but almost.'

He had a nice orderly home. His father didn't do much except smoke a pipe and paint numbers onto bits of wood that he sold to the local hardware store. Now I sometimes wonder if they'd been living off an ancestral family trust or something.

One early afternoon, my sister Debbie and I were in Paul's home playing Monopoly. The day rolled along at a lazy pace; no adults, no sun but calm weather with the lounge window open. We played nicely for a while; a moment I'd have liked to freeze, put in a frame and hang on the wall.

Kids being kids, the serenity didn't last long and a challenge emerged between Paul and me. I don't remember why but Paul was being unfair about something so I wouldn't give him his 200 pounds for passing 'Go.'

'If you don't, I'll throw your sister out the window,' Paul said.

'You dare!' I shouted.

With that, he jumped up to grab Debbie. I leaped up and blocked his way, expecting another hiding but I was outraged he would dare to touch my sister; she was only small.

It was pure luck but I did something that became a regular tactic of mine whenever I got into a fight. As he came toward Debbie, I threw my left arm up and around his neck and curled it back down to my side, which brought Paul's head into a headlock under my armpit. With my right fist, I punched his face several times. It was marvellous. He broke away from me, screaming and swinging at me but missing.

His face, red as a tomato with blood streaming out of his nose and watery eyes, he howled 'Get out, get out,' rushing at us and slamming the door in our faces as we scrambled out.

Deb was right by my side all the time and even at her age, call it primeval instinct, she understood what had just happened. She recognised the reality of challenge versus danger and she saw we finished on top; she was as elated as I was.

I often regarded Debbie as a nuisance, someone I had to include, ever since Peter made me sit and have a photograph taken holding her in my arms. It embarrassed me to be doing this out in public. Peter took the picture of me sitting on a wall by a public paddling pool in Earl's Court and wouldn't let me paddle unless I did the photo shoot. Mum still has the picture today; it looks good; I don't know why I kicked up such a fuss.

Ever since Debbie could walk, she followed me around everywhere but that didn't stop her from finding her own things to do. She was full of imagination and often wandered off on her own, like the time I was over the park with our friends. It was the weekend and a bright, hot sunny day in the park; people scattered everywhere. Well, I realised Debbie was missing; we couldn't find her anywhere. I was beside myself with worry and gut-wrenching emotion and I couldn't go home without her. Fortunately, she turned up after twenty minutes. I knew then how much she meant to me.

We lived on the top floor of our building and there was a fire escape on the back wall that ran straight up to our bedroom window. Fire escapes aren't a health and safety requirement these days however they were then. Anyway, early one morning we woke up with Mr Mitchell climbing through our bedroom window with Debbie in his arms, apologising for waking us.

'What's going on?' mumbles Mum looking up at the window. 'Sorry Veera, I sahw Dehbie she woz swinghen ohn the fire esceepe and I thoght she wuh fuahll, an ah cliembed op an grabbed er foh you.'

We were in shock for several seconds as she climbed back into bed with Mum, then we rolled over and fell back asleep.

Apart from the obvious pride I had felt in sticking up for Debbie against Paul, I realised for the first time that I'd stood up for myself against someone who was bigger than me. This gave me confidence. After a few days, Paul and I became friends again and we never fought after that day. Also, Simon and David dropped their derogatory remarks. I think they realized I could fight back now.

Around the same time, something else happened that gave me confidence. It took place in a dream. I'd been having nightmares since Linda told me about ghosts. She told me ghosts left you alone unless you annoyed them. I asked her, 'How do you annoy ghosts?'

She explained I needed to go into my bedroom and say, 'Ghosties, ghosties, you can't get me-ee, mer mer-mer mer.'

As soon as I got home, I went straight to my bedroom, opened the door, looked in the room and called out, 'Ghosties, ghosties, you can't get me-ee, mer, mer, mer-mer mer, mer. From that night onwards, I had endless nightmares that plagued me for years. I dreaded bedtimes and before going to sleep, I tried to pep talk myself saying 'It's ok, they're just dreams, they're not real.' This continued night after night relentlessly; always the bad dreams and me trying to reassure myself before going to sleep that ghosts weren't real.

But one night I dreamed I was in a large Gothic haunted house, with the typical daunting Dracula style hallway - an intimidating wide stairway curving down from the upstairs floor. It was very gloomy with cold light and two men in dark suits were standing at the bottom of the stairway approaching me with evil intent. Fear gripped me but to my amazement, I looked at them and said, 'This is just a dream.'

They say nothing back but I sense their power disappearing and the whole scene evaporated away and I have a fantastic comfortable and peaceful sleep and wake up feeling refreshed and renewed. The spell has been broken and the nightmares stop right there. Well, at least for a long time.

CHAPTER 12 — Going Up

Something else has happened to me; something that is another amazing confidence booster. I've been in the 'C' stream since the first year of junior school and I'm now in the third year.

I really liked our 3C teacher, Mrs Salisbury, she was so much kinder than Mrs Hunt who had been our teacher the previous two years. There was never any fun in Mrs Hunt's class and it wasn't her strictness that put me off; it was more that she hardly smiled, ever. Even when she did occasionally smile, there was no welcoming sense of sharing; no bridging of the gap between herself and the students. She wasn't letting us in. Her smile reminded me of a radiator grill at the front of a car. On a few occasions though, I was privileged to experience her anger. That was definitely a shared moment with a lot of connection.

One day she was giving the class some sort of physical anatomy education and she asked Linda Daley, to take her skirt off and stand on the desk in her blue navy knickers. It was all very above board and innocent as Mrs Hunt went on with her discourse. Linda was a bit of a bright light and was perfect for the part; she had longish blonde hair, blue eyes and a bit of a mean streak underneath her big wide smile. I thought it was great seeing her in her knickers and I told her, 'Pity we can't see you without your knickers on, Linda.'

Linda was filled with outrageous delight and told me she was going to tell on me and then went straight to Mrs Hunt and told her about my perversion. Mrs Hunt gave me the strongest piece of her mind, as loud as she could, in front of the whole class. I was filled with embarrassment as she fired words at me like 'filthy', 'mouth', 'dirty', 'mind', 'soap' and 'wash.' I instantly visualised Mrs Hunt going to work putting soap into my mouth. Needless to say, she cured me of my open and foul mouth. After that I was very careful with whom I shared my sexy thoughts.

She also stopped me picking my nose and eating it! I don't know how I started the awful habit but I know when I stopped. It was in Mrs Hunt's class. She was reading something from a book; I was sitting at my desk distracted and daydreaming, not really listening and not aware I was indulging in my favourite habit! Out of the blue, I heard my name mentioned. It was Mrs Hunt saying, 'When Robert Craggs picks his nose, he doesn't know where to put the contents, so he puts them in his mouth.'

About half the class moaned out, 'Ughhhh.' I was so embarrassed but was instantly cured of the disgusting habit.

In contrast, Mrs Salisbury, our 3C teacher, was very warm and always had a lovely soft smile on her face. When she smiled, one of her eyebrows would drop slightly at the corner which made her smile look a touch sad. So, whenever she smiled, she always looked compassionate. If it was a child's birthday, Mrs Salisbury allowed that child to draw a big picture on the classroom blackboard. When it got to the month of March, I started to get excited. Just thirteen days to my tenth birthday and my opportunity to draw my picture on the blackboard. I knew what I was going to draw. Someone had shown me how to draw rolling hills, with a few strokes of the pencil and then it was easy to pop a house and garden in and add animals, birds and the sun. I was so excited and when the day, came I went up to Mrs Salisbury and asked, 'Mrs Salisbury, what's the date today?'

'Well I wonder,' she said, 'it might be March 13.'

'Oh,' I added, with a surprised look, 'I think it's my birthday today.'

'Well what do you know?,' she replied, 'Would you like to draw us a picture then?'

I nodded sheepishly as her left eyebrow dropped into a smile and then grabbed the chalk and went to work. It felt great having my work of art up on the blackboard, I think it was warmly received and I remember feeling very accepted by Mrs. Salisbury.

I liked her class and the work was easy. Mrs Salisbury wasn't pretty but I would have hugged her any day of the week. She dressed in a homely fashion and her wavy hair was greyish. She was kind and lovely and I was really mad when Martin Keller threw a bit of hard plasticine at her which got her in the stomach and she made a bad face and had to leave the classroom. He was as rough as guts and was the only boy in our school who I was afraid of and he wore glasses too. I did actually beat him up once but it was a lucky fluke and then a few months later he got me back. He was sitting with Linda Daley when he announced his intentions to me and I think she put him up to it. That afternoon, I walked home with blood all over my school shirt. That was twice she'd ruined my day, although one was on me.

Well it was the first day back to school after the Easter holidays. I'd just sat down in class after having had a great two weeks off and was ready for class. Mrs Salisbury looked at me and dropped her eyebrow. I smiled back and waited for her to start.

Then she addressed us, 'Class, be quiet please. Today is a special day for Robert Craggs. Robert has done so very well in his school studies that he is being transferred up to 3B.' Then she turned to me and said, 'Robert, we all wish you the very best in 3B and we'll miss you but very well done!'

I was sitting there with my mouth wide open. 'When do I go Miss?' I asked.

She looked at me like I was really silly and smiled saying, 'Now Robert, you're going right now.'

And with that, my old class said goodbye to me and I was escorted up to my new class to begin a new and wonderful life.

I didn't have a clue this class transfer was going to take place and neither did Mum. She found out from me, after the event had taken place. The transfer also happened at such a strange time, just four months before the end of the school year. I have so many questions now but at that moment I didn't.

If someone was standing in a queue to board a plane and the flight attendant said to that person, 'Oh Mrs Jones, you've just been upgraded to business class.' Mrs Jones doesn't ask, 'Why?' 'Who made that decision?' 'How was the decision reached?'

I was actually upgraded once, on a flight from Dubai to Perth and I have to say that when the attendant informed me I was being upgraded I gulped, said 'Thanks,' and kept walking before she changed her mind.

That's what I do when I leave 3C. I grab the reins with both hands and take off.

CHAPTER 13 — A Winner

I'm fitting well into my new class; the children are easy to get along with and I'm making good friends. In my previous class 3C, there were a few strong characters who could be very disruptive, negative and difficult to work with. Not so with 3B; the class dynamic is very conducive to happy learning. It's a warm class, full of noise and with vibrant energy. In fact, 3B is the best class of my whole school life.

After a few months, Cadbury invited our class to take part in a Cadbury chocolate essay competition. I think it was a national event. The name of the competition was 'The Milk In Chocolate' and Cadbury would award each class with three prizes in the categories of Bronze, Silver and Gold.

I'd never written an essay before that involved research and we hadn't done any previous lessons on the subject. So, I asked Mrs Walter, my new teacher, how to write the essay. She pointed to the centre desk and said, 'Read one of those books on chocolate and then write what you remember.'

Mrs Walter was nice but stricter than Mrs Salisbury. She had blonde-tinted hair, groomed to perfection and she dressed smart and stylish but in a conservative, classic sort of way.

I found her to be fair and kind but firm and I felt I would not get any more hints from her on essay writing. I walked over to the big round table, picked through the range of books strewn across it and flicked through a few. I felt somewhat lost but settled on a book that had a picture of a cow on it. The book seemed to take the reader through the chocolate making journey but with more emphasis on the milk. One thing I knew; by the time I got to the end of that book, I'd have forgotten the contents.

So, I read a paragraph, focused on the important bits and copied it down but in my own words. If I came across a word I didn't understand, like, 'consumer' or 'extraction', then I would just copy the word down and hope for the best. In some places, I copied the whole sentence, word for word and hoped that my essay wouldn't look like I had plucked it straight out of the textbook. I didn't know what 'plagiarism' meant.

Several weeks later, the results arrived but I knew I'd won a prize the week before. Paul Elijah, the bravest boy in our class, had been rummaging around the cupboards during playtime when the classroom was empty. He'd found a box with several Cadbury's tins and one of them had my name on it. As I came into the classroom after playtime, he ushered me over to the cupboard to show me before Mrs Walter came in.

Seeing that chocolate tin with my name written on it lit me up inside. I hadn't won anything before. Life was showering me with love.

I'd won 'silver' and on the day I received my prize, I went straight home, I didn't want 'hang-out' time with my mates; I wanted to be alone with my prize. It was a big royal blue tin with hints of purple streaked through it. Inside were several bars of chocolate, all different sizes and types; dark, milk and cream filled. It was reminiscent of Charlie from 'Charlie and The Chocolate Factory' who had also received a medal of honour. They filled my 'medal' with delectable delights fit for only the chosen few. I'd been chosen.

I'm in the sitting room, no-one's home but me. It's not dark enough to switch on the light but it's getting there. I'm humming the UK team theme song for the Mexico Olympics by Long John Baldry and I'm soaking up my own glory with my tin of chocolates.

That was 50 years ago and while doing research for this memoir I discovered something I hadn't realised back then; the competition commemorated the 1968 Summer Olympics, hence the bronze, silver and gold categories.

CHAPTER 14 — Miss XL

Paul Winston and Steve Hullett in 3B have become my two best friends. Living down the road from where I live, the three of us often walk home together, cutting through Crystal Palace Park. I leave them at Chulsa and head up the road to my house on Crystal Palace Park Road. Paul Elijah, from 3B, also lives on Chulsa; he's becoming a friend of mine too.

I'd never in my life met anyone with more fearless bravado than Paul Elijah; nothing scared him, not even adults but he was always courteous with them. He knew what adults wanted, what they needed and he'd give it to them, without distraction. With long, dark eyelashes and striking blue eyes, he looked quite the angel but he was far from that. I'd seen him fight before. Inflicting extreme pain on his victim seemed to give him pleasures unknown. He became a good mate of mine for a while and was a natural leader who led our mates and me into many bad situations. He got me to go along to his boxing club, which ended with him smashing up a workman's hut while I headed home on the bus, never to return. I joined his church choir - he had an excellent soprano voice - but that only lasted one night after a bout of car window smashing. Then he persuaded a bunch of us to run away from home with him to Petts Wood in Kent. Paul said we could live in the woods. We'd caught a train there on earnings from 'Penny for a Guy.'

A few weeks before 'Guy Fawkes' night, kids made their guy and stood on the street asking, 'Penny for the Guy?' A Guy was an effigy of Guy Fawkes who had tried to blow up the Houses of Parliament in 1605. We spent the Guy earnings on fireworks and on Guy Fawkes night we burned our Guy at the top of the bonfire to commemorate Guy's downfall and King James's lucky escape. We couldn't be bothered to make a Guy, so we got the smallest of us, Steve

Dunton, to sit on the ground while we did our best to make him look like a Guy by putting a mask on his face and tying his sleeve cuffs over his hands and tying gloves on the ends of the sleeves and putting a floppy hat over his head. If someone didn't give us any money, our Guy called out a cheeky remark, which shocked a few people but never earned us any money. But we made enough to pay our train fares to our 'run-away' destination. As the evening set in, we became cold and hungry and decided to head back to our homes.

Paul had a great range of interests and ideas but no matter which one we engaged in, something went wrong or he'd end the evening by smashing bottles and vandalising public property. I did similar things in my teens but he was ahead of his time and too scary for me, though I found his dares amusing.

Like the time we did the 'Nature Dance' at school. They designed Nature Dance to connect us with nature. Our school was focused on getting us in touch with nature, whether it be mountains, trees or our inner selves. On this day, our class was in the main hall doing an arty nature dance. Our teacher told us to take three or four staccato steps before freezing into a tree-like position. Decades later, Madonna did a similar thing with her song, 'Vogue,' the catch line being, 'Strike a pose.' I tell you; Malcolm Primary School was way ahead of its time.

Well, we had a temporary teacher at our school. A young French female teacher with short sexy blonde hair. This young French female teacher with short, sexy blonde hair dressed hot and her name was Miss XL. Can you believe it? Miss XL. Her name alone was pure tease and she was the sexiest piece of candy a schoolboy could ever dream up. Whenever I saw her, I'd gaze in her direction, hoping for a smile from her lovely blue eyes, shadowed under long dark lashes. To add to her already overloaded sex appeal, she was cool and indifferent!

One afternoon, Miss XL was in the hall helping the main teacher. I was with Paul Winston, Steve Hullett, Paul Elijah, Melvyn Peel and Dane Baxter. We were like jumping beans hoping for a smile from Miss XL. She wore a short black skirt with long slim dark tights and a fitted top with horizontal stripes. We were laughing at each other saying things like, 'You want to kiss her,' 'No, you want to touch her bosom,' 'No, you want to get her knickers off.'

We didn't admit what WE wanted to do; instead, we transferred our desires onto someone else. But then, Paul Elijah said, 'I wanna smell her bum.'

A momentary silence followed that statement. It stunned me. This was a fearless admission of filthy desire, which, by the way, I shared. Paul Elijah was the only 'brave' among us who took ownership of what he wanted to do. He wasn't trying to transfer his fantasy and make it someone else's. No, he was standing up. I imagined wafts of French scent from under Miss XL's dark skirt, when Melvyn cut into my thoughts, mouthing in a hot whisper, 'Go on then Paul, I dare ya, do it.' We all joined in, egging Paul on but he didn't need much convincing. That crazy boy would do anything.

The dancing began. The other teacher instructed us to strike a pose like a tree. 'Reach your arm up and out and step around.' Miss XL also danced around like a sexy extra.

'One, two, three, tree position,' the teacher would call out and we'd take gnarled tortured steps like a tree uprooted and contort our bodies and jut our arms out like warped branches or stand tall on tiptoes and shove twisted fingers up to the sun.

Paul, while doing superb tree impersonations, made his way over to Miss XL. She was unaware she was being stalked by a twisted tree and Paul made it look as if he wasn't aware of her being nearby. He seemed to be absorbed in his art. 'One two three, tree!'

Every time I froze into my new tree position, I tried to make sure I was facing Paul; not wanting to miss anything. He was closer to Miss XL now, pretending to be interested in nothing but his dramatic interpretations. I felt envious! He was near Miss XL and I wished I were near her too. What if she noticed him and gave him a smile? Or said something nice to him? They might elope to Paris. Goodness not only was he about to experience a forbidden pleasure but he was now close enough for a genuine interaction with her. 'One, two, three, tree!'

He was closer now and then in the next few moves, he was behind her with his back to her, deflecting suspicion. Then 'One two, three, tree!' She stepped forward and bent over at a forty-five-degree angle and he stepped towards her and bent down, like a tree drooping by a lake.

He checks the hall to make sure no-one is looking. As he scans the room, he makes eye contact with me. Smiles bust out of my face but instead of smiling back, he looks me straight in the eye; no emotion, like I'm not there. It's as if he doesn't know me, well not as me but he can see right into me. What does he see? A mindless spinning top. I feel shallow; I lack substance. But he doesn't, he's not like that; he's not like me. I'd always assumed we were the same. We've always laughed at the same jokes, always enjoyed doing the same stuff. But here he is; solid, still and aware, as I'd never seen him. I feel uncomfortable realising I'm not like him; that he's not like me.

I'm not ready for this yet. Later, when I'm older, I'll come back and unpack this experience; but not now. Right now, I'm intent on having fun and I don't want to deal with uncomfortable awareness. I snap **out as if breaking** a spell.

Seeing the way was clear and no-one looking, he stretched out his neck toward the underneath of Miss Excel's skirt and for about four seconds breathed in and experienced pure French mystery. I could hardly believe his brazenness, his total lack of fear but he'd done it. He'd done something unbelievable and we were roaring inside with contained laughter and excitement. He had become the Schoolboy's Own.

After the dance was over, we jumped around him like a pack of wolves and he, the alpha, accepted the pleasure of hero worship.

I had a question though. What did Miss Excel's bottom smell like?

'Talcum powder.'

His words left me with a vision of Miss XL, patting French perfumed talc around her bottom before pulling up her French panties.

At nine years of age, that wasn't my first schoolboy fantasy but it was powerful.

It's summer and Paul Elijah is moving to Orpington; just before we're delivered up for slaughter to the local senior high school - a place where we'll lose more of our innocence.

I miss him; but it's good he's moved away.

CHAPTER 15 — As Best As Ever

Life is fantastic at school, both academically and socially. The work is easy and fun and I'm excelling at sport, school projects and whatever opportunity comes my way. But when I share these victories with Mum or Peter, they smile and say, 'Well done' but they're distracted. They have bigger issues of which I'm unaware. I don't realise how unhappy they are together. Even the biggest news yet to come will not raise the roof in my house. It will raise my roof though. Even decades later, it will still lift my lid.

It was the end of the school year and Mrs Walter was having a chat with the class before we left for our six weeks summer holidays. We were excited and itching to get out of class but Mrs Walter knew how to get and hold our attention. I think she enjoyed it too.

'Now class, when we come back to school, I won't be teaching you in 4B.' Moans of sorrow floated up into the air like balloons.

Next year I'll be teaching 4A.' More moany balloons, 'Oh Miss!' So far, her tone had been formal but then her tone changed. When Mrs Walter was sitting on good news and was holding it back with suspense, she would slowly amble up and down the aisles between the desks where we were sitting. Then she would stop and balance her left shoe on its heels at an angle and slowly rock it forwards as if she were about to step forward and then change her mind and rock the shoe back again. Forward back, forward back. Sometimes she'd twist it gently to the side. It was as though she loved this left shoe of hers and her ankle and wanted to show it off to us. She was doing it now, just one aisle away from me.

'But,' she continued, 'there are three children here, in this class, who will be joining me in 4A.' She stopped again and tested her shoe heel. Is it possible for a silent room to become several times quieter? Oh yes! The air changed and the room became static. If she had our attention before, it was now stretched to breaking point. We honed in on her like a pack of sheepdogs, eyes keen, waiting for the whistle, a facial gesture or a clue to signal our next move. There wasn't even a micro-sound. Mrs Walter was enjoying this suspenseful moment. Her creation. To her, it was music to dance to. Her front shoe, on its heel, was doing the side stretch.

'So, I will announce the names of the three children who will join me in 4A.' Here's the moment.

'Paul Winston, Steve Hullett and Robert Craggs.'

I felt the slow Mexican wave washing over me. She stood there smiling and continued, 'Everyone has worked well this year but these three boys have shown excellent progress.' She said more things but I blanked out as I visualised myself in 4A, the top class in the whole school. I heard my name being mentioned. She was looking at me seriously.

'I particularly want to congratulate Robert who only joined our class a few months ago from the third stream. Some of you here might be surprised to see Robert going up into the 'A' stream but he's worked hard and has earned his passage. Well done Robert, you should be proud of yourself.'

For a moment, I wondered whether she was doing me a favour because she was fond of me. My school report had been a good one but I had only achieved middle ground in maths and English, the two most important subjects. Was it because I'd excelled in sports and class projects? I'll never know. I didn't have questions as I do now but I was more than happy. I'd risen from 3C to the top of 3B and was heading to 4A, the best and top class in the whole school. And I'd achieved this momentous leap in just three months.

If this was a movie, it would best end here. This would be a perfect moment to have the cameras panning away from my beaming smile; Mrs Walter standing behind me on my left squeezing my shoulder. Paul and Steve standing next to me, chuckling. A handful of kids in the background applauding, nodding their heads to one another in joyful approval and the headmaster Mr Jenner coming up to shake our hands and patting me on the head and saying something funny to me that no-one can hear; a private joke between the two of us; I say something back to him and we both end up laughing. And as the credits start to roll, there'd be music in the background; the Beatles, singing 'All You Need Is Love.'

My life couldn't get any better. Record screeching to a haaaallllt… and it doesn't.

CHAPTER 16 — A Crack

The momentous news of moving up another stream at school seems to go unnoticed at home. Mum is struggling to pay the rent and Peter's not around much. The summer holidays pass by and before I know it I'm back at school, in my new class, 4A with Paul and Steve.

We're even more bonded now in our new environment. We are the new boys and at first, we cling together like boy scouts in a jungle. But we soon dissipate like ink dropped into water and we make new friends.

Within a few months of getting back to school, Peter left. He was the kindest he'd ever been on that day. I was at home; don't know where Mum was. I walked into the living room to find him sitting in the armchair all dressed up smart. He called me over and put his hand around my shoulder, this being the first time he'd ever handled me in a caring way.

'I'm going away for a while Robert; you won't be seeing me.' This news surprised me but I liked it. I'd never felt cared for by Peter. In fact, I feared him, he had no idea how strong his hands were but I did and I've seen the blue flashing stars. I didn't want him to see I was happy with this news, so I cried. He pulled me onto his lap, hugged me and said things like, he'd been under pressure and one day when he got back, we'd go fishing. I nodded in the right places and then as soon as convenient jumped off his lap and ran out to play.

I was too young to understand that his support enabled Mum to get me out of foster care. Mum was a beautiful catch; but a catch with a price; me. I remember how happy Peter used to be when we got our first place together in

Earl's Court. He was always singing, 'I Like It' by 'Gerry and The Pacemakers.' But the happiness didn't last.

How grateful was I for his contribution? I wouldn't call him 'Dad.' I couldn't. Anyway, I wanted Mum to marry Roger Moore. Most people will remember Roger Moore as the third James Bond but in his earlier career he played Simon Templar in The Saint. Simon Templar was handsome, dressed smart, spoke well, had good humour and could fight well too; a tough act for Peter to follow.

Four years they stayed together; four years and one baby girl, my sister Deb. Deb believes Peter's dead now. He hadn't a clue how to look after himself. He lacked discipline and a sense of responsibility and care, even towards himself. But if it's any consolation, Deb carries his genes and she's a beautiful girl with two lovely daughters. The best of Peter lives on through them.

When he left, Mum felt her life falling apart. She thought it was 'Game-Over.' Not long after Peter left, I woke up one night to the sound of wailing and sobbing. It was distressing, so I got out of bed and crept into the sitting room and there I saw my mother sitting in an armchair. But I'd never seen her like this before. She looked at me as if I were a stranger; me, her son! She looked wet. Her face was wet. Wet with tears. Her eyes were wet. Even her hair looked wet.

I needed to get to her; had to get to her. I needed my mum; needed to close the gap between us; to hold her. I needed her to hold me; to reassure me. I needed contact with her; with her skin. I needed to smell her, to have her surround me with her arms and her skin. I needed to be in the middle of her, to have her hold me; hold me with her arms and tell me everything was ok. It was the only remedy and I needed it, I needed remedy from Mum. But Annie

Stewart was with her. Annie was caring for her. Mum seemed to need her. She didn't seem to be aware of me. How could she with Annie guarding her? I wanted Annie out of our way.

Annie took me back to bed. 'It'll be ok, go to sleep.'

But it wasn't ok. Back in bed, I still heard Mum's distress.

I wanted to wrap my arms around someone or something but all there was, was a cold, dark, damp hollow space. I lay there with my arms wrapped around myself and curled myself into a small ball with my legs tight up to my chest and sunk into a spiral blackness of vivid dark dreams; my first experience of fear and despair.

I don't think I went to school the next day; or did I? Annie took care of Deb but not me and I have no idea why I couldn't stay with them but it was cold and terrifying at home, so I sat on the hallway stairs hoping Mrs Stewart might notice me and welcome me into her home. That's where Debbie sat, by the warm fire, with food on the table and cartoons on the telly. I wandered up and down the corridor, in my own blackness, feeling abandoned.

Mum came home around 4.00pm. I was hanging around Stewart's hallway when she showed up. She smiled and seemed happy to be home. Seeing her, I welled up inside with relief. She had bandages around her wrists. I couldn't understand why she'd cut her wrists. I could tell by her smile she was glad to be home with us but I had wondered why she did it. Was it because we were wrong; because I was wrong?

Debbie, seeing Mum, chatted away like a little bird, as if Mum had only been out of the room for ten minutes; Debbie, with her snotty nose and unbrushed hair, dragging her foam giraffe around, with half its neck missing.

Mum soon picks herself up and life gets back to normal; a few friends rally around but I think she has the wrong friends. Valium helps; so does Bushy, who brings a lot of laughs into our home with his antics. Then comes spring and with it the news; we are moving to Chulsa.

This is where I began my story: The story of moving onto Chulsa.

It's a happy time; but not without dark shadows; nevertheless, there's hope. Even in the shadows.

CHAPTER 17 — Italian Blood

We've moved to Chulsa. Deb has the measles and is in bed while I'm exploring my new territory and playing with Paul and Steve. Steve lives in Agate, the next block to us and Paul lives down the bottom of the estate in Ripley. Fancy living on the same housing estate as my two best classmates! Steve has converted me and Paul into fellow Manchester United fans. He has George Best on his side who is now our hero. George Best will become the first of a long line of controversial players who play great football but lead more than colourful lifestyles the tabloids love to share. I've badgered Mum into buying me a Manchester United football kit. The top is long-sleeved red cotton with a white crew neck and white wrist cuffs; the shorts are white nylon. I hardly ever take it off.

We played over at Crystal Palace park at the top end by the small lake. It's a big open spot of about five acres of well-maintained grass that circles around about 80% of a small lake and slopes down to it. Behind the lake is a stage where there would be occasional rock group performances. I've seen Bob Marley there, David Bowie, Lou Reed and many others and neither I nor any of my mates ever paid a penny to get in. We knew that park and all its fences, bushes and holes and no security man or his dog ever kept us out. But I'm getting ahead here; back to soccer.

Usually, we'd put one player in goal and the other two players played against each other and the first to score a goal would replace the goalie. On this day we played two against one. Paul and Steve against me. We set our goal posts (rolled up jackets) at each end of our imaginary pitch. I didn't think I'd have much chance because not only did I have to score against them and defend my goal but they were better players than me.

They came against me, confident of an easy defeat. Paul passed the ball to Steve and ran forward, towards my undefended goal, expecting Steve to kick the ball to him. But Steve wanted the glory of dribbling the ball passed me. This worked to my favour. I tackled Steve, got the ball off him and found myself racing straight up the hill towards their goal. This was another handicap for me. Not only were they both better players than myself but I had to run uphill which was a greater struggle than their downhill picnic in the park.

Fortunately, Paul had run down to my goal hoping for Steve to pass him the ball which he planned to pop into my undefended goal. So, when I had taken the ball off Steve, Paul was comfortably out of my way, many yards behind and he'd never catch up but Steve was right on me. 'Man on,' as they say.

Steve and I were about equal speed with running but I had to run and still control the ball which wasn't easy. I resisted the temptation to kick the ball at the goal straight away as I was too far away to ensure a score. I needed to be closer. Steve was right on my heels and gaining ground but the goal was open with no defender, just a few more steps and I'd be able to kick that ball in with ease. I became so excited with the taste of victory that I started laughing, which may have robbed me of concentration. I lined up my shot to pop the ball in when Steve did the unthinkable! That lowdown rotten piece of scum dived forward and rugby tackled me down to the ground. I could not believe it, I'd been robbed!

His foul outraged me and I let the universe know it. He had broken the moral code of fair play. And he knew it too. At first, he fell to the grass rolling around laughing, trying to tell me how sorry he was. Paul was laughing too as he made his way up to us from my goal where he'd been hanging out for a pass. Steve knew he'd done wrong but he did a clever thing. He brought his friend George Best in the equation. 'Rob, even George Best would have done that.'

I wasn't having it; George Best would never have committed such an outlandish foul. What made me so angry was that they could have let me have my well-earned victory rather than denying me my moment.

They awarded me a penalty. I still didn't think it a fair trade but I took the offer. I aimed the ball far right towards the bottom of the goal and kicked it as hard as I could while trying to maintain foot control. It wasn't a great shot but I got a swerve on the ball and it curved toward the bottom right corner but that blasted Steve anticipated the ball, dived right over and saved it. Steve and Paul burst out in joy and I burst into tears!

The injustice overwhelmed me. He hacked me down and then he saved my penalty. Where was God!! They tried to humour me but I felt betrayed.

An hour or so later Paul, Steve and I were standing near my house by the road barrier which cuts off Amberly Grove from our estate. We'd just got back from the Crystal Palace Park where they'd just cheated me of my soccer victory. I don't know how the conversation started but Paul and Steve were talking about my skin colour, in a tone that suggested misfortune. Skin colour? Wasn't it bad enough that they robbed me of scoring my goal earlier on? Oh, if I could have lived that moment again, I'd tell them both to get stuffed. Instead, I tried to reason with them that I was only a bit brown. But they held their ground; I was still brown and brown is not white. I thought they were dumping me as their mate and I saw my world crumbling away and began to cry again. That was twice in one day.

Moving to Chulsa

They were sorry they'd made me cry again and our friendship didn't seem in jeopardy but I felt separation. They had something in common, something I didn't share.

I told my mum about what had happened. As if she could fix it? Funnily enough, she did. She told me that my father Assefa was half Ethiopian and half Italian. This had something to do with the Italian occupation of Ethiopia during WWII, which brought many Italian soldiers and personal staff into Ethiopia. That meant I was only a quarter black. Why that's nothing at all! And it made me feel much better about myself.

She's lying of course. I'll find that out when I'm in my mid-thirties. She'll blurt it out in tears that my dad isn't mixed race at all. He's a full-blooded Ethiopian. Mum will keep this going for years because I often moan about kids teasing me for being brown. But I believe she's doing it for both of us.

I'm not the only one with low self-esteem.

CHAPTER 18 — Assefa Berhane-Selassie

I don't think about my father much. Up until the age of six, I believed he was dead, then Mum told me he was alive and living in Ethiopia. It was strange having a dead dad who was now alive. Images of black kin in loin clothes with spears running around the jungle. Little do I know that he's living in Sweden with a family of his own.

After leaving my mother, Assefa moved back to Ethiopia to work on an electrical dam project, which resulted in him going to Sweden to do a course. There he met Aila, a Finnish refuge who had moved to Sweden after the Second World War. They got married and Aila gave birth to Saba. But their marriage only lasted five years.

Assefa's story is unusual. From a young age, Haile Selassie had him raised in his household yet when Assefa grew up, he became involved in trying to bring down Selassie's government. Why?

The story goes back several generations. Haile Selassie made Ethiopia a strong African nation by taking over surrounding kingdoms and creating a union. This was a necessary political move to strengthen Ethiopia and prevent colonisation from the many European nations racing for a piece of the African pie.

Selassie called himself 'King of Kings,' a quote borrowed from the Bible. He didn't mind the other kingdoms having their own kings and feudal lords; at least for a while but he knew true strength lay in unification and he saw himself as their King of Kings.

One of these kingdoms, the largest, was the Jimma kingdom in the Kaffa region from where coffee originated. Several generations of kings had ruled in Jimma, starting

Moving to Chulsa

with Abba Faro in the mid-1700s.

By the mid-1800s and under Abba Jiffar I, the kingdom converted to Islam and remained that way for the next several generations. Abba Jiffar II was their last king in the 1930s, when Haile Selassie seized Jimma.

It's not clear whether Jiffar II had sons but he had grandsons. His grandson, Abba Jofir (my granduncle) revolted against the annexation and tried to seize the throne from Jiffar II who was turning senile and had become Selassie's puppet. Selassie responded with military force and imprisoned Jofir in Addis Ababa.

Not long after this revolt, Selassie removed Jiffar II from power and elected his own son-in-law, Ras Desta Damtew, the new governor. Jiffar II remained king but he had no real power. When Jiffar II died in 1932, the kingdom of Jimma became part of Selassie's Ethiopian empire.

Jofir was a strong character and risk taker. He tried to revolt against Selassie but was unsuccessful and ended up imprisoned. His brother, Abba Bilo (my grandfather) was more amenable to Haile Selassie's political seizure. Selassie even adopted Bilo into his family as his godson which meant Bilo and his family had to leave their Islamic faith and convert to Christianity. Selassie also changed Abba Bilo's name to Kegnazmach Berhane-Selassie; this new name reflected his new identity as a Christian and member of the Selassie family. Kegnazmach also had to relinquish a part of his land. Selassie rewarded him with a government post; a sop if you will.

Not long after, Selassie had Bilo's brother Jofir imprisoned, Italy invaded Ethiopia and Selassie and his entourage fled, first to Harar and then to Kenya. The Italians then released Jofir from prison and appointed him as their governor. He became useful to them, helping with Italian propaganda broadcasts to the Arab speaking world. In return, the Italians gave him a bodyguard of ten armed men; a privilege not given to many Ethiopians.

After Italy's defeat in 1942, Selassie returned and sent Jofir back to prison. It's not clear when, possibly the late fifties but Selassie gave Jofir an amnesty. Jofir spent his remaining years living in his old crumbling palace in Jiren; constantly under watch.

My father Assefa, born in 1937, was the son of Kegnazmach, Jofir's brother. On returning to Ethiopia, Haile Selassie took over Assefa's education and sent him to school along with the sons and daughters of other nobles. During those elementary and secondary school years, Selassie took Assefa to live with Colonel Tamiret Yigezu and that's how Assefa came to be in the Selassie household.

I assume Assefa's father, Kegnazmach, was unhappy with how the political situation had changed his circumstances. Both Kegnazmach and his brother, Jofir, had much of their land confiscated. Haile Selassie himself may have been responsible or it may have been his corrupt government officials. One administrator suspected of this land theft, Ras Mesfin Sileshi, denied the allegations, claiming he'd inherited the land from his wife, who also had legitimate claims to the properties claimed by Aba Jiffar and his descendants. Assefa and many inhabitants of the Kaffa province and many other parts of Ethiopia held negative attitudes on this alleged form of usurpation by the Ras. Also, many of Jiffar's descendants looked unfavourably upon Assefa's father, Kegnazmach because of his conversion to Christianity and his passive acceptance of Haile Selassie as overlord, in contrast to his brother, Jofir who stood against Selassie.

Assefa had a loving relationship with his father but he also maintained a good relationship with his uncle Jofir and that part of his family. Also, Colonel Tamirat Yigezu, who Assefa stayed with during his schooling years, replaced the Ras as governor and did much to rehabilitate Aba Jofir and his family. He also helped them recover land that the government had taken from them. Assefa claimed the government had seized a large area of land from his father, though he didn't show much interest in pursuing those issues and seemed more interested in working for the general development of his country.

I believe a mix of emotions influenced Assefa to turn against Selassie; brought up under the Haile Selassie household while his other family members suffered outside that circle; the bravado reaction of his uncle compared with his father's passivity; and the unjustified seizure of property from his family. The seeds were sewn at an early age.

In the early fifties, Selassie chose Assefa, among other students, to go to England for further studies and he attended the University Of London. He graduated in 1956 with a degree in engineering and then worked with Standard Telephones and Cables Limited in London, leaving England in June 1958, just three months after I was born.

When my mother met Assefa in London in the mid-fifties he had already become interested in politics and was in a political movement aimed at bringing Haile Selassie's government down. After he and Mum separated, he returned to Ethiopia and became involved in an electrical engineering programme as an inspector for the Ethiopian Electrical Light and Power Authority which involved building the Koka dam. It was an important Ethiopian project which

Selassie came to visit. It's interesting to note my father had great reservations about Selassie at a time when he was occasionally in close contact with him.

In his younger years, Assefa was a member of the Ethiopian Student Association and he investigated and proposed different reforms for his country. These reforms were considered by the ruling classes but were then rejected. Over time, the association grew into a strong and radical movement and became the building blocks for many of the political parties that exist in Ethiopia today.

While Assefa was on a course in Sweden in 1960 he became involved in a coup d'état on Haile Selassie. Assefa publicly joined with the Ethiopian Ambassador of Sweden, Ato Terefi Sharew, to show support for the coup. But the coup failed and all involved were exiled by the Ethiopian government.

Assefa sought asylum and made Sweden his home. He settled down into family life sometime around 1963 but his heart was forever in his political activities. The Ethiopian Student Movement eventually gave birth to the first political organisation called MEISON, the All-Ethiopia Socialist Movement - a communist organisation. Apparently Assefa was one of the founding members though I didn't find evidence of this in my research.

Mum tells me many stories about my father. Night-time is when she talks of her past; perched on the edge of her settee; coffee mug filled with sherry; it pours out. She tells me my father is related to Haile Selassie the emperor of Ethiopia and that my father comes from a wealthy family that grew coffee. The Ethiopian government took most of his family's wealth. She also tells me how Assefa had been trying to bring down the Selassie government. These stories don't add up but they fascinate me. Nevertheless, it's all so far away from my life on a council estate in south-east London. I enjoy listening to these tales of my ancestry but during the day I leave it all behind as I try to fit myself into the daily life around me.

CHAPTER 19 — Reverse Charges

Paul and Steve remain my best friends until Steve moves away which leaves Paul and myself in an unsettled state, neither of us assuming leadership. We've always looked to Steve as our natural leader. Both Paul and I liked him best, he was bright, easy to get along with and funny but he had an unusual leadership style. Or maybe not. He led from behind, like a director. Paul was the shyer out of us, so I was the one out there being directed. An unpaid star who thought he was leading. Like the time we; no not we but I, got into trouble with Julie at school and made me look a complete fool, all because Steve had a bright idea!

I knew Julie from Mrs Marsh's class when I first moved to the area. Mrs Marsh, the fat fluffy marshmallow, with a hard-slapping hand; delivered to my legs on more than one occasion.

Many years later when I became a hairdresser, who would walk into the salon where I worked? Mrs Marsh! I had a panic attack seeing her and feared she might again take my leg and deliver another reminder of who the marshmallow was. She became a regular client at Mates Hair Studio and we'd often chat together; once I'd gotten over the initial shock. It turned out that her poor son Andrew had developed mental health issues.

The day she shared this terrible news with me and Dawn - my most favourite salon colleague – Mrs Marsh sat in the styling chair with a coffee and biscuit on her lap waiting for Graham, my boss, to come and put rollers in her hair. Dawn and I sat around her sharing in her grief while she sobbed, saying she 'didn't know what to do.' It seemed natural that in between sobs, she'd sip her coffee but what struck me was that during her sobs, she managed to take her ginger biscuit and pop it into her mouth, crunching away with sad gusto. It looked bizarre, her eyes showing sadness while her mouth chewed away in obvious delight. I couldn't help noticing a deep contrast between the top and the bottom of her face. Her eyes weepy and sad as willows but her mouth couldn't care less. I didn't dare look at Dawn.

Getting back to Julie. She was bright, bossy and confident; the class leader; out of bounds for me, Paul and Steve. Her dad was a policeman and they lived in a proper house, not a flat and she had a telephone. So did we; at the bottom of the street. She had straight blond hair with a strong blunt fringe and sharp blue eyes. The government could use those eyes for national defence. I don't know how I ended up with her phone number but I had it and when I left school on Friday afternoon, with Steve and Paul walking beside me, I called out to Julie, 'Have a nice weekend Julie, see you Monday,' she called back smiling, 'Yeah see you.' It must have been the afternoon outdoor games; she and I must have been thrown together in something fun. Is that how I got her phone number? Who knows?

On our way home from school, Steve, Paul and I were excited that Julie, the class star, had become our new friend and we were eager to develop that friendship; but how? Steve had a plan. We'd telephone her. But we had no money. Not a problem. Steve had the solution, 'We can reverse the charges.'

I'd never heard of 'reverse charges' before and I didn't know it meant the person we phoned picked up the bill. Early Saturday morning we walked down to the bottom of the estate to the telephone box. We crammed ourselves into the red kiosk with its dozens of little square windowpanes; some smashed by vandals. Stephen picked up the phone and dialled 100 and asked the operator if he could make a reverse charge call and then he gave the operator the number while we waited. I didn't know what was happening; that the operator was asking Julie's father if he wanted to take the call. After a few minutes, the operator told Steve that the caller was accepting the call. Then Steve shoved the phone into my hand to speak to Julie's dad.

He wanted to know who I was. He didn't sound friendly. In fact, he seemed cross. This wasn't a great start for my relationship with Julie. He wanted to know why I wanted to speak to his daughter. Was I a friend of hers? Why had I made a reverse charge call? He told me people should use reverse charge calls for emergencies only. He told me he was a policeman and he told me off. Then he told me that this one time I could speak to Julie but I should never use 'reverse charges' again for social calls. I agreed. Then he passed the phone to Julie

'Hello Julie, it's Robert'

.... 'Hello.'

'What are you doing today?'

..........................'Nothing.'

'What's she saying?' Steve butted in from my side

'Shh!'

'Do you wanna come out?'

...................'No, I can't.'

'Is she coming out, ' Steve again

'Shh, I can't hear!' I hissed.

'Oh well, I'll see you at school on Monday then?'

.... 'OK.'

'OK bye Julie.'

'Don't hang-up yet,' Paul butting in.

'Bye,' she hung up.

Well, the phone call was short and I had every reason to be disappointed but I felt elated despite Julie not wanting to come out with us. At least I got to chat with her over the phone; that was a first. And she had agreed that I'd see her on Monday, so I hung onto that as a good thing. Steve and Paul shared my optimism and when Monday came, we walked into school together excited with anticipation.

I looked forward to seeing Julie, hoping to become friends with her; special friends. I imagined that I'd be closer to her than Steve and Paul and it would be true justice for me to get the blond blue-eyed girl. That would teach them for making nasty comments about me being brown.

As we approached the cloakroom, Julie was there with her girlfriends. I smiled but she didn't reciprocate. Instead, she made her way towards me, too directly I feared. It wasn't good. Nor was that look in her eyes. Then came a verbal assault hurled straight at me; so articulate and well charged, I couldn't hold ground and couldn't muster a defence. Steve and Paul who had been right by my side shrank behind me into invisibility. I was on my own for this one but not Julie. She had the weight of her entourage. She stormed into me and I stood there with my mouth wide open in mute embarrassment.

Words, like air missiles, came flying at me through the air. 'How dare,' 'who do you think?' 'Don't you' 'I was so,' 'My father' 'My house?' 'I want nothing.' 'If you ever.'

I couldn't duck; there was nowhere to take cover. So, I stood there getting caked in the verbal mortar. Then, when she had finished, she turned on her heels and marched off to class, followed by her female comrades, some of whom gave me a discourteous back glance before skipping off to catch up with their leader.

A few lone witnesses standing around like actors in the wrong play stood looking at me, confused, wondering what hideous crime I had committed before realising they might be late for class. Then I noticed Steve and Paul materialising from thin air. I was relieved to see them and I showed my gratitude with an accusation of my own.

'Well that was nice wasn't it, leave me to take the blame!'

'I didn't, we were right here, weren't we Paul?'

'Well I didn't see you, you just let me take the whole blame!'

'It wasn't our fault Rob that Julie just had a go at you.'

'Yeah if I was in front, it woulda been me.'

'Yeah well it should have been you, it wasn't my idea to reverse the charges.'

Steve just gaped at me without words. Stuck.

'It was all our fault,' Paul pushed in.

'Yeah,' Steve echoed, relieved.

'Well how comes I got the blame?'

'I dunno.'

Silence, then, 'Shoulda seen your face Rob,' Steve was

trying to contain a laugh.

Paul was smiling and I tried to put on a brave smile. If it had been Steve or Paul who'd taken the fall, I'd have been peeing my pants. But it wasn't any of them, it was me and I didn't like being the fall guy.

We tried to work out a solution. How to fix the 'Julie' problem but we couldn't find one. I wasn't mature or confident enough to apologise to her and I seemed to remember her suggesting that I don't go anywhere near her. On top of this, when Peter, my stepdad left us, he had left something behind. You see, Peter had a terrible stammer and one could easily go off to the kitchen, make a cup of tea and come back before he finished his sentence. But when he left, he left me with his stammer. So, I wasn't feeling very comfortable about trying to make amends with Julie. Any stress, frustration or excitement would reduce me to a stammering mess. Instead, I pushed the memory away, like it never happened and I never so much as looked at her again.

Sometimes I notice her from the corner of my eye but I never look at her and I'm sure I don't exist to her. It's funny how some people can spend so much time in the same space without acknowledging one another; like some married couples. We sit at different sides of the room. All the kids between us.

CHAPTER 20 — Heading North

It's not only the end of the school year but the end of junior school altogether; neither Steve, Paul, nor I have passed the eleven-plus, the final primary school exams. So, there's no grammar school for us. We have a few choices for secondary school, the main ones being Kentwood or Kelsey Park. Paul said he's going to Kentwood and he's my mate so I've told Mum I want to go there too. She's fine with that.

But with the end of the school year, the summer holiday arrived and with it the soft easy weather and carefree days. I spent most time playing over at Agate House, in and out of Steve's with Paul. We played records, soccer, even strip poker; my grandparents came home and discovered us half naked. They were cross but said nothing and I was relieved at not having to explain myself.

Days rolled into each other with the sun softly glimmering through the shaded chestnut trees; it seemed like one long continuous day. Steve mentioned that our local soccer team, Crystal Palace, who we didn't support, had moved up to the first division. This meant Manchester United, who we did support, would be playing our local team, which meant we would get the chance to watch 'Man U' play locally. Steve said his dad would take him and would I'd like to join them? I asked Mum and she said yes!

The match was on Saturday 9 August 1969. An overcast, heavy summer day; it matched the slow, congested traffic. Crowds of hopefuls, smiling with expectation, spread out along the pavements and over the roads. Cars resigned to their fate crept along slowly in jerks and starts. Dozens of road vendors littered the streets selling football scarfs, hats, t-shirts, hot dogs and cans of soft drinks and we walked past them with pride, wearing our football kits for the occasion. I'd never been to a match before and didn't know what to expect but I assumed we would be sitting down with plenty of space to watch the match.

I was in for a surprise. We had to stand on a bus at rush hour packed in like tinned sardines. Still, we had a reasonable view of the game and it blew me away seeing George Best and Bobby Charlton running around in front of us and before I knew it, I was shouting and cheering my head off. After the match, Steve's dad let us hang around the changing rooms to wait for the players to come out and we got loads of autographs from both Crystal Palace and Man U players on our football annual books. That's my last memory of being with my good mate Steve.

About a week after the match I travelled up to Newcastle for a two-week trip to visit my grandparents. When I returned, Steve had moved away to Orpington. I used to go up north to Newcastle at least once a year but on this trip I travelled alone. We always said we were travelling to Newcastle because Newcastle was the nearest city. But my grandparents lived in a small town called Birtley, just south of Newcastle. My grandparent's home is where Mum was born and we'd been travelling up there for holidays ever since I can remember and before.

Travelling alone excited me. I'd board an evening coach at Victoria Coach Station, setting off around 10.00pm with a packed supper, comics and books in my bag. My big case would go in the storage compartment below. The bus drivers with their Geordie accents were my first contact with the new world I was entering. They weren't just drivers, they were ambassadors; boarding their coach was like stepping onto Geordie soil. Children today get excited about going to Bali or the US for a trip. Well, for me, traveling 'Up north' was an event!

I loved going up north and I've always loved the Geordies, even Billy Skelton who beat the crap out of me the first time I met him. We were play fighting over the park in the early evening; the noise of kids all around as they jumped on swings, ran up and down the slides, screaming and shouting. My cousin Dave Robbins had just introduced me to Billy. Dave and I weren't really cousins; our parents led us to believe it for whatever reason. Anyway, Dave was supposed to watch out for me. As soon as he introduced me to Billy, Billy decided I was Cassius Clay and he was Henry Cooper. I liked this arrangement as Clay was the superior boxer and this meant I would win. But when Billy pinned me down to the ground and began punching my lights out, I knew I'd been played and couldn't see my big cousin anywhere.

Billy Skelton – Skella - was a rotten scoundrel but I still smile when I think of him. He gave me a tattoo once, standing out by his garden shed; Indian ink and a pin; a cross right on my forefinger. I was so proud of it; a mark of initiation carried out by the worst scumbag in the area.

I would think of him and others, as I journeyed up north and wonder who was hanging out with whom and what we'd be getting up to for the next three weeks.

As our coach cruised through the streets of West London, I'd play a game in my head. As the coach headed along the streets, I would look for where the transition between urban roads and the countryside took place. Where did it happen and would I witness the change? I never did; the change happened too gradually. The small dense high streets would open out to an occasional dual carriageway, only to become small high streets again in other smaller towns. After ten minutes there would be the bigger freeways curling around above us, then roundabout after roundabout and then I'd notice the towns were further apart; everything becoming larger, industrial. Then, there it loomed before me, the A1 motorway.

My next head game, as I looked out into the dark night, lit up by motorway night lamps and occasional farmhouse lights, was wondering in which street does a person's accent begin to change? Would one town or village be the dividing line between the London accent and the next one, say Northampton? Is there an area where it's unclear what the accent is? Maybe a bridging town with a bridging accent? Where on the map did the Birmingham accent kick in? I imagined it would be before we arrived at Birmingham but how much before? What about the divide between Lancashire and Yorkshire? I wondered if there might be somewhere near the joining borders of these shires where their accents would blend into each other. Some houses at the edge of these shire boundaries looked lonely and I couldn't imagine anyone wanted to live in them. I felt sorry for them. I imagined how it would be to live in the last house by the border; lonely on the edge of nowhere. Desolate and with the wind always blowing and it would never be summer but always winter. And if summer, then too hot.

I spent most of my holidays in Newcastle and I always wanted to be a Geordie; either that or an American. Didn't everyone want to be American? When I was with my Geordie mates, I would speak Geordie all the time. Well, as best I could and no-one told me I was doing a rotten job. 'How man how'z it gannin?' 'Way how are yeh?' 'Way I'm up for coople of weeks man and then I'm gannin back yem.' I loved pretending to be a Geordie, it was as if I was someone different; someone else, someone other than me.

I used to think of the Geordie dialect as a lazy way of speaking but it's not. A dialect is a language and the Geordie dialect is much closer to true old English than the modern standard English spoken today.

After the Romans left England, the Anglo-Saxons overran the area followed by the Danes and they left their language as they absorbed themselves into the community. Later, the Normans invaded England and the French language became the main language spoken, while the English language went underground for 300 years before re-emerging. As it is today, the Geordie dialect is about 80% Scandinavian and Anglo-Saxon, which is as about as close as we can get to the old English language. The modern Standard English of today is about 30% Scandinavian and Anglo-Saxon with a 70% mix of French and Latin. So, if a Geordie comes up to you and says, 'How man, lets gan doon the toon and deck soombody,' he may be speaking with offensive tones and of unruly desires but he's using the best and oldest English to do it.

So anyway, I'm still on the coach travelling up north to see my grandparents. The coaches back in those days didn't have toilets, so there would be two 20-minute stops along the way to go to the toilet, get refreshed, grab a cup of nasty tea and lose money on the fruit machines. I always loved this part of the journey, still do. The stops would be around midnight and early morning. I loved being out late with everyone back at home sleeping in bed, while exploring the night in the middle of nowhere; a half-asleep motorway cafe, with a few people travelling to various destinations; a couple of elderly ladies, a young nurse, a mother with two children, a young soldier in uniform heading home for a break. Someone would put a coin in the jukebox and Neil Diamond would start singing about his 'Sweet Caroline.'

Moving to Chulsa

Motorway cafes in England never have quiet downtime these days. They're a hive of activity, day and night. Gone are the lonely counters with a cup of weak tea and an emaciated sandwich. Enter bright franchise businesses competing with one another for our attention, serving food and drink to our heart's delight. 'Would you like that with soy? Extra shot? We have organic. Would you like it toasted? Warmed? What type of bread? Would that be all?' 'Would you like a quick shag under the counter?' 'Have a great day!'

I like the choice and service offered today but I miss the half awake, half-trained locals working under poor lighting; my old life is being replaced.

Our coach would arrive at Chester-Le-Street bus station around 6.00 am. Chester-Le-Street is a market town just a few miles south of my grandparents' house. Being summer, it would have been light for the past two hours; a bluish grey light with lots of early morning mist. I usually walked from the bus station to my grandparents, it took about 45 minutes. Everything was quiet and still with hardly any cars or people about; a big contrast to the urban life in London and all the houses looked different, all built with local stone and brick. What hit me though, was the smell, especially as I got closer to my grandparents' home. They and most of their neighbours lived in small council houses with adjoining front and back gardens with low fences, each with a large vegetable patch and the pungent stink of greens, cabbages, earth and horse manure. It was an odour which at first affronted my nose; strange but I wanted more; I would try to catch it again and breathe it deep in. It had a sense of goodness about it and I came to associate it with hard work and goodness.

My grandparents' house lights would be on and in the

cool morning I'd knock on their door; no-one in that area had doorbells. The tradition up there was to bang on the door and call out the name of the person you wanted to see. Bang bang bang, 'Robert!'

After a warm welcome, Nana would put the kettle on and make tea and teacakes and we'd sit and talk for a while. Grandad asked questions about Mum and life down south while Nana showered love and kindness over us with food and drinks. As I grew older, I became aware of often saying 'No' to Nana, 'No thanks, I've just had breakfast,' No thanks, maybe later.' 'No, I've just eaten thanks.' But I'd get fed up of saying no and resigned myself to putting on the damn five kilos.

Most of my mates up there never moved far away from their original homes but I've lost contact with most of them. I'm still able to contact a couple though and they sometimes fill me in on who's living where and who's doing what.

My main mates were Paul MacDougal – Macca and David Robbins - Ropper, not to mention Geordie, Davey, Boots, Mouse, Skella, Roo, Fritz and Smaalley.

After breakfast, I would go around to Paul's house as he lived nearest. It would still be early but none of my mates knew I was coming, so I needed to catch them before they went out for the day.

Unlike my grandparents' home, Paul's house, like most of my mates up there was in need of some TLC. The garden sheds, fencing and gates needed some repair and apart from the veggie patch, there wasn't much thought about aesthetics; not many flowers, plants or shrubs. Most of the mums and dads looked a bit rough and ready and Paul's parents never smiled. Not at me anyway. Most of the men drank hard and most of the women accepted their lives would never reflect the Hollywood images they'd once seen at the movies. Some of them looked at me with a strange curiosity and I never understood why. It was only later that I made guesses.

Even though I came from a broken family, I felt like a prince in that hard area. As I walked up to Paul's door, I was always excited, imagining how excited he'd be to see me. I'd knock on the door, bang bang, 'Paul!' I'd do this a few times before Paul would eventually get out of bed and open the door. Then I would feel let down because these Geordie lads never showed delighted surprise. Paul would look at me for a few moments without the slightest look of surprise or joy on his face at seeing his old mate. Then he'd ask, 'When ya ganing back?' Not how long are you here for but when are you going back? Actually, my mates up north were pleased to see me but they were a dryer bunch than I was used to and so I learned to just accept and slip right into whatever was happening at that current time.

I think I was privileged to be an occasional part of the northern life. It was a life though, that I only took part in, in recurring snapshot moments. Let me give you an analogy.

I read a book by Oliver Sacks who is a physician. He studies brain function and he wrote about one of his patients who had been blind but through modern technology got his eyesight back. Scientists noticed, through studies of him and other blind people who had received sight, that people need to learn to see and one of the biggest problems for blind people who receive eyesight is learning to see motion. What we don't realise is that our brains visualise motion in thousands of miniature pictures, like the old-fashioned movies. But because of the enormous number of single picture images we process, we don't notice any jerkiness; instead, we see a smooth singular motion. But for people who have only just received sight, it's different. They see motion as disconnected stills and the effect is unsettling. To the new-sighted, a car driving along the road would appear to jump in staccato movements.

It made me think of my visits up north. When I say goodbye to my mates up there, I leave them playing innocent games at the bottom of the golf course in the early evening dusk. When I return several months later, I expect to pick up where we left off, only to find that the gang had changed and are no longer hanging at the golf course but now play at the slag heaps. Sometimes I'm disappointed but I have to roll with it. I begin to realise that the north isn't staying the same. It won't wait for me to return before continuing on again. I can't put it on 'hold.' My alternative reality where I am a different person isn't under my control. It carries on without me and I have to jump back into wherever it now is, whether it's the playground, golf course, army cadets, snooker cafe, pub, club or disco.

CHAPTER 21 — Stepping Into Agate

I'm back home after my trip up north and I've called on Steve. I've been looking forward to catching up with him after my holiday. But to my shock, he isn't there. Instead, a new family has moved in – the Collins family and they know nothing about Steve or his family. Panicking, I run home and ask Mum if she knows where Steve has moved. She doesn't and I don't think she realises that I'm in a state of alarm. This is serious. I ask around but no-one knows or cares. All anyone knows is that he's moved to Orpington. Orpington! I hate Orpington and I always will; too many old mates moved there.

I found it hard to accept that Steve had left without leaving his address; no contact, no word, no goodbye note; he just disappeared. It was so wrong and out of character and it left me at a loss. One of the great things about moving to Chulsa was being with my best mates. If the universe had moved me to Chulsa to be with my mates, how could Steve go? The math was wrong.

For a while, I lost direction. There were other kids at Agate whom I knew but I didn't feel on as good terms with them without Steve. As for my other best mate, Paul Winston, who lived at the bottom of the estate? Well, even though Paul, Steve and I had hung together as a trio, Paul and I didn't fit together for a while. We would become good buddies again but with Steve gone, we had a re-settling to go through.

So, I drifted towards the Agate group. About that time, a boy moved into my block on the third floor, Terry Goods. He was a rough looking lad and he scared me a bit.

Over at Agate, there was a family there called the Hanks

and I was in love with both Jane and her younger sister June. I had often hoped to become noticed by either one of them. My efforts were in vain. Jane seemed a quiet girl but superb at pack management and it pleased her no end to drive the pack against me.

Somehow she instigated Terry to fight me. I don't know how she engineered it but having to fight him terrified me. He stood there looking at me, ready to pounce. I had one option; hit him first and as hard as I could. It surprised me but the tactic worked and Terry burst into tears. I couldn't believe my luck; this hard-rough looking boy just stood there crying his eyes out. Jane's plan A hadn't worked, so she resorted to plan B which was to tell on me. The next thing I knew, Terry's Mum was in my house talking to my mum and I was getting a sound telling off. But Jane's Plan B didn't work either, because Terry's Mum suggested that Terry and I shake hands and makeup, so we did that and became great mates.

He and I both shared the same desire of winning Jane's love. So ok yeah, I was a slow learner. Jane liked Terry but she seemed to enjoy making my life a misery. More fool I for taking it but alas I was in love with her pretty face.

The Hanks family was the 'in' family. Mr and Mrs John and Jean Hanks were a gorgeous looking couple and their three kids, Jane, June and John weren't wanting in those 'good looking' genes either. When 'hot pants' came into fashion, Jean, the mother, jumped straight into her pair and she looked like dynamite, though it was Terry and me who were exploding. Mrs Hanks, hot pants and pubertal lust were a volcanic mix!

Terry and I were envious of Mr Hanks; we'd imagine him watching TV at night with Mrs Hanks cuddled up against him in her hot pants. We became distant hero worshippers. We even ditched our football clubs and supported Everton soccer club because Mr Hanks looked like Alan Ball, the Everton soccer club captain.

Many years later just before moving to Australia, I received a phone call from an old friend, Edith, one of the crowd who lived in Bailey House and who had been an ongoing friend of Jane Hanks over the years. She passed on an invitation for me to go to Jane's fortieth birthday party. I decided to go along and looked forward to catching up with the old crowd.

The party was in the Bell Green Social Hall. Edith couldn't make it and apart from Jane, there wasn't anyone there from the old days and Jane and I didn't have much in common, so our chat was limited. I headed off to the bar where a grumpy old fella sat making grunts at me. I asked him what his connection was to Jane.

'Er Dad,' he said, not even looking at me; he didn't like wasting words or syllables. But his brusque manner didn't put me off; this was Jane's dad, a hero of old and I told him so. I told him how he had been a distant hero of mine and Terry's, just by being beautiful Jane's dad and how envious we were that he was married to Jean; with her hot pants and how we even ditched our team and followed Everton just because he looked like their captain.

Well, he and I ended up spending the whole evening there at the bar steeped in intoxicated nostalgia. Mr Hanks, John now, if you don't mind, became louder and more gregarious and by the end of the evening had a smile on his face as big as a Cheshire cat. He even became generous with his syllables and his sentences became longer by the hour.

I left the party around 9:30 pm. It was twilight; lots of cars on the road; people heading out for the evening. It felt good; the Saturday night energy filled the air.

I thought about Jane, how self-conscious she appeared earlier that evening when we chatted; she had looked uncomfortable as if she was wearing an ill-fitted dress. We had an exchange of niceties, our words like pawns, sent forward to feel the way. She was guarded and I tried to make a joke about our past; a sacrificial attempt to lighten the air and bridge the gulf between us but she saw threat and recoiled and so we pretended what was wasn't and what is, isn't.

As I drove up Sydenham High Street, I realised I had been gloating. Before leaving, I had sprinkled the party hall here and there with droplets of my life; family man, beautiful wife, healthy smart children, thriving business, lovely home, nice car, Australia. It made me realise that perhaps I hadn't gotten over my childhood interactions with Jane. I tried to think of something nice about her but I couldn't think of anything. The best I could summon up was our occasional quiet group moments together; Sunday afternoons on the garage roof listening to the top 20 on Terry's transistor radio.

There are several of us sitting on the roof, listening to the hit songs, like, 'Love Me Love My Dog,' Tom Tom Turnaround,' 'Me and you and A Dog Named Boo' and 'Indiana Wants Me.' During these moments, a momentary peace settles over us as we rest under the shade of the giant oak tree, tall and sturdy with its widespread leafy wings, keeping us safe for a while.

CHAPTER 22 — Bobby

There's a block of terraced garages opposite our flats, the front right corner of them is fifteen metres from my balcony. It's set into the front of a hill which slopes at the back down toward Agate House. So, whereas the front of the garage is too high to climb, it's easy to walk up the bank on the right side and slip onto the roof with ease. There's a long waiting list to rent a garage; someone has to move away or die to create an availability; having a garage is a status symbol.

Bobby Cohen was one such person. He was about 16 when I met him. I was about 11 years old. It was his dad's garage but he was always out there with his oily rags and greasy spanners tinkering with his motorbike. He had mid length greasy dark hair, blue eyes, acne and soft bum fluff around his face like he was trying to grow a beard but his beard couldn't be bothered. I think he liked us hanging around marvelling at his shiny bike. As long as we knew he was king.

'I like your bike Bobby.'

He'd let my comment hang in the air. Then, after a few minutes he'd say something about the engine that I didn't understand; Something about 2-stroke.

Both Terry and I nodded our heads in agreement.

Then he'd pull out his rags and polish up the metal, saying with a fatigued expression, 'Chrome, man it's the only way to go.'

Terry and I would nod in wonder at this revelation. One day he showed me his knife. Disappointingly, it didn't flick up through the handle but instead flicked out with a swing from the side of the handle. I don't remember where he got it from; maybe a day trip to France. With a half grin, he said, 'I've sharpened it on a metal bar. Could cut your throat with no pressure.' He held it up menacingly in front of my face.

I stepped back, 'Cor, don't Bobby'

He grinned, satisfied.

I was impressed; it made me think of New York gangs. 'Bobby, can I have a go?'

'Piss off.'

One day he showed us his lighter. It was a metal petrol lighter. Wind proof too.

'Try and blow it out,' he said.

I tried but I didn't blow very hard. I didn't want to blow it out and show him up. My role was to be in awe and to be fair, he had awesome stuff. He had a motorbike, a flick-knife and a lighter and he told us he would take us over the bombsite to show us how to smoke.

The bombsite was in Amberly Grove opposite the back of our house. The whole length of Amberly Grove was one huge bombsite. Within a few years it would become a housing estate but for now and since WWII after having been bombed during the war, it had been fenced off with corrugated iron and designated a derelict area. The rest of the houses were pulled down and were overgrown with weeds, trees and shrubs. There were a few underground bomb shelters too which we loved exploring; a quick hop through the fence.

It was a beautiful Saturday morning and the early sun was shining in between the trees, littering the ground with textured shadows and there was no school till Monday. I felt so grown up that I would be smoking with my mates. We got through the fence and found a bomb shelter. We bent the corrugated iron back and nestled ourselves half-way down into it. Bobby got his lighter out and snapped off bits of dry grass; real dried out grass weeds. 'This is natural and wild tobacco,' he said, 'We're gonna smoke it like the Indians used to.'

This was more exciting than I thought. I was about to smoke real grass tobacco. Forget the cheap cigarettes my mum smoked; this would be the real stuff that tribal people smoked. Bobby set the end of the thick strands of grass alight and then blew it out and sucked the smoke down his throat. He coughed a bit and then passed it to Terry. I have to say, Terry looked a pro, even if he pulled a face. He looked like an adult enjoying pain. He passed it to me. When I sucked the smoke inwards, I was shaken by how my throat rejected it before it got anywhere near down my throat. The burning sensation stunned me and my eyes watered like a fountain as I nearly lost control of the coughing fit. 'S'good.' I lied.

Neither of us came back for anymore, I don't think smoking weeds had a great appeal but it was good having been a part of this secret smoking society and as I walked back home on that beautiful morning, I felt different, like I'd changed. I'd been initiated into something unspoken.

I used to think Bobby Cohen was a bit dangerous but that didn't stop me becoming too familiar with him. Our friendship soon ended. He was working on his bike and had gone into the garage to get something. Terry and I had been standing around with him and we thought it would be fun to play a little trick on him. It's funny how these things happen. A spontaneous idea. Who started it? Don't know. Whose idea? Don't know. A look? Raised eyebrows? A smile that says, 'Shall I? Yes?' And before we knew it, we had locked

Bobby in the garage. It was only fun; but boy did it backfire. I expected him to simply call out, 'Ok, guys, you got me, the fun's over, come on, open the door.'

We received a very different reaction. What we got was Bobby Cohen screaming at the top of his voice, 'Open this fucking door, 'Open it now or I'll break your fucking neck.'

He was screaming so loud, I panicked. He was screaming out the foulest of things he would do to us unless we opened the garage door immediately. I reckon the whole housing estate could hear him. I wanted to run away and leave him there. Go home and switch on the TV. But I'd be in serious trouble and he'd hunt me down and stab me with his flick-knife but if I opened the door now, surely he'd beat me to a pulp.

I chose to carefully let him out and run for my life. He was screaming about cutting off my testicles and cutting my throat, I was scared out of my wits. 'OK Bobby, I'm opening it' Terry had abandoned me and was about ten yards away.

The garage door was one that lifted up and slid backwards. I slid it up and as I did so he ran out at me and I took off as fast as I could but he swung at me and caught my ear. It hurt but I reckon I got off lightly. I screamed anyway to make him feel better. His face was as red as a beetroot and I realised I'd hit a nerve. I think Bobby was scared of the dark.

We stayed away from him after that and he seemed to slide from view and thankfully he didn't hunt me with his flick-knife.

A little after that incident, I learned something about Bobby Cohen which depleted even more the hero worship that I had had for him. There was another garage area up in Charleville Circus, which was up the hill, joining onto the top end of our estate. We had discovered an old abandoned car up there that had been stripped down of everything except its body, steering wheel, seats and wheels. This garage area had a long sloping driveway running down between the garages and Terry and I would push the car to the top of the drive and take turns rolling it down again and steering it. It was great fun and we did it every day after school and weekends. We soon attracted the attention of a big boy who we hadn't met before. His name was Brian Newley who lived in Bailey House, which was between my block, which was Beacon and Agate. He seemed nice enough and he took an interest in us and hung with us for a while. The conversation turned to Bobby Cohen. He could tell I was scared of Bobby. He asked me, 'Are you scared of me?'

I shook my head, 'No.'

'You sure bout that?'

'Mm.' I nodded. I wasn't scared of him, he wasn't scary.

'You're scared of Bobby Cohen but you're not scared of me?'

'Mm.' I nodded again.

He smiled to himself and shook his head and repeated, 'You're not scared of me?'

'Uh uh.'

'But you're scared of Cohen!' He said the name like it had a nasty taste.

'Yeah.'

'What if I told you that Cohen's a coward and runs away

from me? Then would you be scared of me?'

'Uh uh'

'But you'd still be scared of Cohen?'

'Yeah.'

He smiled again, shook his head and said, 'I don't get you.'

I'll soon discover Brian is someone to be reckoned with but I can tell he isn't a bully. Cohen is. I'll soon discover Brian has a younger brother John and him, I will fear.

CHAPTER 23 — Brother John

We're playing up at Charleville Circus in the derelict car and have been getting to know Brian but while we're rolling down the hill, his hand rests on the wing mirror. The car steers too close to the garage wall and there's a noise as metal hits stone, followed by a scream. Terry lifts his hand and stares at the gash; his face turning white. He runs away, lightning speed, like a homing pigeon to his mum, cradling his hand like he's holding an injured bird; all the while letting out a long continuous deep siren wail. He has to go to hospital but he's ok, though for years later that part of his hand will become bright purple and will be painful during winter months.

We didn't see Brian after that but his younger brother John Newley would sometimes grace us with his company. Whereas I liked Brian, I was uneasy around John. Like Bobby Cohen, he was a couple of years older than us and looked down on us. But unlike Bobby, he was sure of himself. Goodness knows why he hung out with us, he didn't like us. He had a Norse look about him, with a long nose which he looked down over to steer his vision and he hardly ever smiled. If he did, it was barely visible; mostly inward like he was sharing a secret with himself.

During the summer holidays, we discovered a terrific bike track up nearby the sports centre in Crystal Palace Park. It wasn't a purpose-built track, we didn't have things like that back then but it was great for what we believed was dangerous cycling.

The previous Christmas I had been given a bike as a present, from Aunt Viv and Uncle Ted. I had been begging for a bike for years and nearly died a death when I finally got one. It was a second-hand bike and not at all flash but it worked and that's all that mattered.

The bike track weaved in and around trees and shrubs and it took several minutes to complete a circular route. It felt good and exciting, like I was on a motorbike, skidding and kicking up dirt. Me and John were trying to get around the course as fast as possible. I was about a half minute behind him giving it everything I had and as I came skidding around a corner I nearly rode into him. His bike was lying down and he had his back to me, 'Fucking hell John, what are you doing?'

He flashed me a hard look and I knew something was up. I tried to see what he had in his hand but he kept his back to me. 'Shut up and keep quiet.'

'Ok John but what is it,' I whispered.

I still didn't get an answer, so I craned my head around to get a better vision. I saw the reason for the tension. He was rummaging through a lady's handbag.

'You got a handbag John' 'wheredya get that?'

Without turning he said, 'Found it.'

'Where?'

He ignored me as he swept through the contents. Then he stuffed something in his pocket and threw the handbag into the bushes, 'Come on, let's go.'

I never knew how much money he'd found in that handbag, he never said but cycling home, he asked: 'wanna go to Battersea Fun Fair tomorrow?'

'Yeah!'

I felt sorry for the lady who had lost her handbag. I had

Moving to Chulsa

a picture in my mind of what she looked like: Brown eyes, pale skin and thick soft dark wavy hair, long. And she'd be wearing a dark brushed woollen coat. I imagined her husband or boyfriend walking home with her through the park, holding her hand, consoling her over her loss. She was the innocent and I was the guilty. She belonged in The Garden Of Eden. I chose Battersea Fun Fair.

I called for John about nine o'clock the next morning like he had told me to. 'Guess what,' he asked, 'My mum gave me a shilling for making my bed, she said I'm a good boy.'

He let out a light smile. Not much. Measured.

So off we trotted; John with a pocketful of notes and me hanging on for the freebies. We went on ride after ride. They had this ride called The Rotor which spun around so fast it stuck me to the wall and then the floor moved away from my feet, I couldn't tell if I was upside down or sideways.

The sun shone and songs like 'Layla,' 'Spirit In The Sky and 'Something', belted out through the air. I couldn't get over Johns generosity, he even bought me burgers and drinks and candy floss. I began to think that perhaps he was a good bloke after all. But that would often happen. I'd think he was OK but then he'd say something real nasty.

We were standing in a queue for a ride alongside an Indian family. John sneered and said, 'I hate Paki's, they smell. Can you smell them, I can?'

I couldn't smell anything but I didn't dare admit it; I was on thin ground here. If I can't smell them, then maybe that's because I'm one of them. He was looking at me.

'Oh yeah' I said, as I scrunched my nose and pulled a bad face.

'See,' he says, 'I told you.'

Beneath his still blue eyes, that are studying me from above his long nose, I catch the faintest smile. Hardly visible; but it's there. It makes me feel uncertain. He is a bastard after all.

CHAPTER 24 — Fight

A new boy has moved into Agate House. His name is Peter. I'm over there and I don't know what's gone wrong but the gang has turned against me and Jane is adding fuel. Peter's Nan has come down to sort things out. She's trying to grab me by my shoulders to tell me off for whatever it is I've done wrong.

In frustration, I turned and hit her in the chest. I think I was more stunned by what I'd done than she was. I'd hit an adult, a lady at that and an elderly one. In shock, I turned and ran home with the whole posse right on my tail. They chased me right up to my front door. Mum came out to see what the commotion was all about. The crowd was shouting atrocities while I stood there bewildered, tearing up.

Then Peter's Nan just came up, put her arms around me and hugged me, 'it's OK, I know you're a good boy.' I sobbed into her tiny frame. Then she said, 'You call me Nanny. Nanny Winters.' And with that, she became my Nanny Winters and the crowd dispersed, disappointed; no lynching today.

After that, Peter became my friend. But I was fonder of his nanny. She was tiny and plain and had long thin grey hair that she tied into a tiny knot on top of her head and she wore an old shabby coat all seasons, day or night. She lived with Peter's family. I loved going into their house as she always made me coffee and toast. Whereas I liked Nanny Winters, I didn't like her grandson, Peter, much. He was spoiled. He had everything. Even both Jane and her sister June were his girlfriends.

I would have gladly swapped my life for his. I would have moved in and kicked him out. This was a dark period for me; I resented his lack of appreciation for everything he had in his life. If you've ever seen the movie or read the book, 'The Talented Mr Ripley,' you'll know where my poor head was. I wanted his life.

One thing though that Peter and I enjoyed together was playing soccer and when we were playing, we were at peace. His Uncle Kevin who lived on the estate down at Chalmers House also played a lot with us. He was a married man with a little girl but he was always out playing soccer with us. It never occurred to me that he may have been slouching on his duties as a father or husband but he was a fantastic coach and gave me a lot of confidence in myself as a player. He taught me and Peter how to kick a good cross from the corner position, how to use the inside and outside of our feet for ball control, how to get the foot under the ball to give it lift and how to get the ball to swerve. We called it a banana kick but now it's called 'bending it like Beckham.'

As I improved in soccer, so did my self-esteem and for a while, Jane began to be nice; I thought perhaps she fancied me, so I wrote a love letter to her and June, her sister.

'Dear Jane and June. I love you. Will you be my girlfriend? Please write yes or no in the box.'

I drew a few love hearts and put a few kisses on the letter and put it in an envelope, then I put it in their letterbox late afternoon just before tea-time. Not long after, their reply came. The answer was yes. The two most beautiful girls on Chulsa Housing Estate were now my two-girl harem.

I sat around the whole evening dreaming of walking around the garages, sitting under the oak tree and walking around the bomb sites, holding Jane's and June's hands.

The next morning, I got up way too early and called on Jane and June. Normal people who weren't in love were still in bed asleep. Jane and June were still in their pyjamas when I knocked, so I hung around outside in the cool morning air waiting for them. We walked around a bit but they didn't say much. I guessed they were feeling shy around their new man. After ten minutes they made an excuse about having to go indoors for their breakfast, so I called on Peter to break the bad news to him.

He took the news rather badly and stormed off crying to get his nanny. She came to the door and after listening to Peter's accusations, tried to explain to him that sharing was good and it would be good for me to have one of the sisters as my girlfriend. Then Peter blurted out 'But he's got both of them!'

Nanny Winters seemed stuck for a moment as if she'd just discovered a fishbone in her tooth. Then she suggested, 'Well, maybe when Robert's had a turn, he'll give one back to you.' She was looking at me with a hopeful smile and I returned with an uncertain nod, hoping my turn wouldn't be too soon. Peter stomped off sulking to his bedroom with his soccer annual.

Jane and June couldn't come out after breakfast, as they had to tidy their bedrooms, so I went home for a few hours. When I came back, I couldn't believe it. The whole crowd was sitting under the oak tree, including Peter, June and Jane. Peter came running up to me shouting, 'Guess what, Jane and June are my girlfriends again' Jane gave me a hard flash of her eyes. A cold realisation settled over me. I'd been played, betrayed and exposed.

I hovered on the edge of the group, not sure of my place. Jane would whisper into someone's ear while looking at me.

She was either concocting something or trying to rattle me. These situations usually ended up in some uproar.

Well, a fight did start but this one was without Jane's meddling. John Newley had wandered over to us and he and I got into a fight. I'm glad we did because he was big trouble and a nasty person and the fight we had separated us permanently from one another. Over the years, I managed to get myself into enough trouble without John's help but I think it would have been worse if he had been around influencing me.

I still don't know how the fight started. A harsh remark, a challenge? Who knows but John and I are up on our feet facing each other. He's got amusement written on his face. He looks confident like he's enjoying this. I'm not smiling. I'm wishing I could turn back time and replay the bit that got me into this messy situation.

All the kids are up on their feet, startled. The air has changed, I can smell it. There's an energy in the air. I catch a look on Susan Collin's face. It says it all; shock, excitement but also dread. Dread for me. I want out. I want to disappear into thin air but there's no getting out of this. The only way out is through. I could run but running away would be worse than getting a hiding. They'd shower me daily about my cowardice. That'd be a lot harder to bear than a bloody nose, a few bruises and a black eye.

But as I face up to John, I have a weird sensation in my backside; I'm empty and weak. John allows the hint of a smile to show. He knows he's going to make me sorry and everyone knows it. I bet Jane is looking forward to seeing me humiliated. Well, I'm not going down that easy. I look for an opportunity, an opening. He's taller than me, he's got a longer reach and he has the killer instinct. I don't have these things.

So, I must trick him. I try feigning an attack by pretending to lunge for his left side but then switching to the right. The move unbalances me like I'm trying a new dance move not yet invented. Either that or I've got cerebral palsy. This is embarrassing and psychologically it's already one-nil to John. This is not a good start. Then I remember the move I made on Paul Fisher. It won't be easy; John's tall but it's worth a try. So, as John and I move closer together I jump up at him and manage to get my left arm around his neck and as I come down to my feet, I bring his head down into a headlock. His head is wrapped under my left arm and then with my right fist, I swing as many punches as I can into his face.

All my fear has gone; converted to adrenalin. All I want is beat the crap out of him. This is a lucky break and I want to make it count. I become aware everyone is shouting and screaming. I can hear my name being shouted. A couple of dads quickly descend on us from nowhere. It's Susan's and Perry's dads. They jump over their lounge balconies to get to us. It's the first time I've ever seen Perry's dad in his singlet. He's muscly.

John's nose is bleeding but it's understood he is the bully and I am the underdog. I'm relieved it's over but I wanted to finish him. For the first time ever, John's got the biggest smile plastered onto his face but it's not real and he keeps saying, 'I can't feel a thing, I'm not hurt, I can't feel a thing, he didn't hurt me.' The dads send him off home and the Agate crowd jump around me. I'm a hero. Susan keeps saying to me 'I didn't know you were such a good fighter' And I'm lapping up the praise. Jane reads the crowd and concedes that this is my day.

About a week later John Newley is with his mate by the sheds. He comes over, calls me a nigger and punches me in the face. I go crying to my mum and she chases him down the road. You should see her; setting pins and clips in her hair, chasing two big boys. I feel loved when seeing her do that. It's almost worth the punch in the face.

CHAPTER 25 — Second Biscuit

I'm expanding my territory, after all, I've got my bike and I'm becoming more confident with it. So, Terry and I spread our wings and begin moving away from the Agate crowd. Problem is, my bike often breaks and needs repairing. Fortunately, Terry's dad is good at fixing bikes, so I'm often knocking on his door, standing there with my broken bike and a hopeful smile.

They had a two-bed flat on the third floor. Terry's mum and dad shared one bedroom while Terry and his big brother Jim shared the other. Jim never talked to either of us or looked at us. I think he lived in a different dimension. Their bedroom wasn't just a bedroom, it also served as their tool shed, complete with workmate, vice, pots of screws, washers and anything you'd expect to see in a tool-shed. That's where Terry's dad would fix my bike; in their ten-square-metre bedroom.

It was a very male household; his mum, so passive, so easy, so amenable; unable to feminise her home, unable to have any womanly influence over any of her men. The poor lady was almost not there; slowly vanishing under vapours of male testosterone, like an absent-minded tea lady wandering around a mechanic's garage. But she seemed to accept it.

I think Terry could do as he pleased at home, lick his plate, leave the table without asking and probably burp without saying, 'Excuse me.' What freedom! The only freedom we had was being able to dunk our biscuits in our tea but not if we had company. I discovered another freedom of Terry's; one which wasn't allowed to us as children and I wore my burden like a saintly garment.

One afternoon, Terry came down to our place for afternoon tea. Mum put on a nice table spread and we sat around enjoying ourselves munching down sandwiches. Mum suggested I get the tin of biscuits out to go with our cups of tea. Now I have to say, we didn't have great table manners but one thing both Debbie and I knew was that when offered a biscuit, when offered anything in fact, we were only to take one. It was impolite and greedy to take two or more. That's like sin and brings great shame on the family. In fact, I think it might have been worse than sex outside of marriage. Annie Stewart had been having sex outside of marriage and she never got told off for it.

Anyway, Debbie, Terry and I were hovering around the tea table and I offered Terry a biscuit. He took one; so far so good. But his hand lingered and for a moment it looked like he wanted to grab a second one. As his hand hovered - over what was now a prohibited area - he became aware that Debbie and I were staring at his hand as though it had suddenly gone gangrenous. It was like he'd just suddenly developed extra sensory perception. He was aware of wrongness in the air; that perhaps his hand might be moving into an etiquette abyss. And he was in discomfort about his hand's disobedience.

I developed ESP in an instant, the wrongness of the situation flushed adrenalin through my body; every sense in my body heightened. I could see Terry's hand, Debbie's expression and even my mum's mounting unease, all at once without looking and Mum was sitting behind me somewhere.

The atmosphere was so tense; Terry knew the second biscuit was wired to something wrong. He knew he was about to set off an explosion but it was too hard for him to resist.

He grabbed that second biscuit with a quick guilty movement and retreated, avoiding all eye contact. The shock of the bomb reverberated through the room and everything went into slow motion; Debbie, staring at me; me turning to stare at Mum, expecting to hear words of prophetic doom; and then to my surprise and relief, she adjusts the way she sits on the edge of her settee, takes an uncomfortably long puff from her Kensington cigarette and makes a half nod in our direction. She had seen but she had let it go.

Let it go! Bit late for poor Terry. That poor boy sat in the corner of the room crunching into his biscuits with the guilty look of a dog that had just let off the nastiest flatulence known to man. He never joined us for tea again after that. I'm not sure if I even invited him but if I had, I'm sure he'd have been too busy cleaning his bike or something.

When out playing, Terry often knocks on our door for a glass of water. Turns out he's developed sugar diabetes; sure, it's nothing to do with the biscuits. One day, his dad will leave the family. His mum, Pat, will get dementia. She'll die in her early sixties. Terry and I become distant but we keep in touch until I move to Australia. He comes to my salon for haircuts and he's often outside Mum's tinkering on his car and we chat when I visit her. He dies from diabetic complications in his mid-forties. So young.

CHAPTER 26 — Angela and Pat

We can't afford many treats like jam; but we like sugar on toast. We toast one side of the bread under the grill, butter the other side, sprinkle sugar over it and pop it back under and gaze at the sugar melting and glazing across the surface of the toast.

If you think that's bad; we hated brown bread and only ate white and took two sugars in our coffee and tea which we drank from our childhood years onward. We never turned BBC2 on, (way too highbrow) hardly ever tuned into BBC1, (still too highbrow) but always watched ITV (very lowbrow and way up our alley). I dread to think what we'd have been like if we'd had the opportunity to watch TV all day and go on the internet 24/7 to play computer games on iPads and iPhones. With today's distractions, I'm not sure what would have become of us. We didn't have the discipline to measure up to today's temptations.

So, with the lack of distractions, Debbie and I played. We played a lot of hide and seek; we played circus tricks, not one of Deb's favourites. We played card games, draughts, Ludo, Dominoes and Monopoly.

We often slept in the same bed and I'd tell Debbie dark evil stories about the Ice Queen. Then I'd tell her that if she fell asleep, the Ice Queen would come and turn her into ice. Then I'd go off to sleep and leave her trying to stay awake and alive.

I also taught Deb how to play chess; Irish Pat taught me. He was Angela's live-in lover across the road in Burton House. Angela, a close friend of Mum's, was a most unusual lady. Unlike everyone else on the estate, she'd had a middle-class upbringing with private education but she was the black sheep of her family. She was over-emotional and overweight. She felt unattractive and unaccepted by her family and peers and she rebelled in her teens and ended up becoming a single mother living on our council estate with her Irish lover.

But she was a lovely lady with a huge, passionate heart. When she spoke, her privileged background became obvious, not that she was posh. It's just that most of us on the estate were common by comparison. But poor Angela; she was hopeless at life. She never had any money; her house was the worst kept ever and she was always so miserable with her love life; always bemoaning to Mum about Pat. Pat was the irresponsible type and didn't seem to know how to show love to Angela. He didn't know how to make her feel secure.

But when Angela would run away to her mother for a day or two to escape and reconsider her life, that wouldn't stop Pat coming over to our house to look for her. He'd be drunk and carrying a long sharp knife, which he intended to kill her with. He'd be standing at our front door, having great difficulty standing still in one spot. From his wavering, you'd swear there was a heavy wind blowing through the landing. 'Whersh Anshla?' I can see the knife in his hand tucked in his pocket. I'm scared that if there's no Angela to kill, he might stab me instead. 'I don't know where she is Pat, she's not here,' I say, as nice as pie!

His eyes are fixed on me as he wobbles around, like a puppet on a string, 'Ka shpek-ta Veera?'

'Mum's out Pat.' I reluctantly confess; concerned he might push his way in and take me and Deb hostage.

But taking hostages is not what he wants. 'Ya-goe ssiggrette?' He asks.

'No Pat, I don't smoke,' I lie.

With that he slurs something which I think is supposed to be a joke, coz he smiles a bit and laughs, so I smile and laugh too and he staggers out into the evening. I go back to watching TV, relieved I haven't been diced into pieces.

Poor Angela, she was the most passionately unhappy person I knew. She was always talking about getting her life together; she was going to kick Pat out; lose weight; get herself a decent man; confront her eating addictions and quit secret eating in the toilet. When she was miserable, she was miserable but after a good sounding off with Mum, she always felt better and ready to tackle the world again and her food cravings.

But she was also such an open and accepting lady; she embraced life and loved watching operatic dress rehearsals but was also just as happy being in the pub with her man. And she was as generous sharing her happiness as she was her misery. It would be normal for her to come over to our house for two hours just to tell Mum she'd lost half a stone and that her sex life was back on track again. When in these moods, she was just about singing and nothing could bring her down; she became the star of her own opera, tossing her head back and seeing humour in everything.

I used to babysit for her when they went out, which was sometimes three times a week. Three pounds and very easy money but I hated doing it as I preferred to be out with my mates, not stuck in her flat with her little Glen screaming the house down for his mother. Also, her place wasn't just untidy or messy or even dirty. That's how I'd describe my home. Her home was multitudes worse. 'Feel free and help yourself to anything in the fridge Rob,' she'd say as she waltzed out into an evening of wonder and fun.

'Thanks, Angela,' I'd reply, from in front of her TV but I could hardly bring myself to even touch anything; her kitchen was a war zone, I never understood how she could prepare a meal in there. Every work surface in her kitchen was littered with dirty dishes, cutlery, letters, opened and unopened, magazines, catalogues, damp towels, open jars of jam with mildew, half-empty tins of beans with clogged spoons inside, open bottles of milk sitting on the bench top at room temperature.

The sink, like a volcano, erupting a lava of dishes up and over everywhere. It was operatic chaos; bills, crumpled clothes and shoes. It was synonymous with Angela's life. Her life was chaos; filled with drama and colour. Metaphorically speaking, there was more music in her life than most people I knew.

I see now how wonderful she was but back then I saw Angela as the quintessential failure and I tried to keep my distance in case I caught it off her. I had my own issues to deal with and I didn't want to be tainted with her woes. I was growing into a selfish person. I was doing naturally what many of today's 'self-help' books suggest; which meant staying away from losers.

This selfish nature developed and lasted for years, even after I became a Christian and when I got married, in my thirties, I didn't want Angela at our wedding, which was a late request from my mum. Mum, quite rightly, gave me a sound telling off, calling me a hypocrite and a spiritual snob. How right she was. I relented after a few days but too late; Angela had made other arrangements.

I regret that. Angela was a much richer part of my life than many of the people who came to my wedding. With all her flaws, she was a rich and colourful lady and she had a very warm soft heart. She died a few years ago – some terrible diabetic condition, which led to one of her legs being amputated, then more complications. She had a hard life but she never became hard.

Sometimes when I babysat for Angela, her fella Pat would hang about, sometimes for an hour or so before getting himself out of the house. It wasn't easy trying to find a pair of socks in Angela's house; especially when slinging back cans of lager. Pat was an alcoholic but what amazed me was how his personality changed after just a few sips of beer. He wouldn't become nasty but this Walter Mitty would emerge. Pat was a short and light guy, with dark hair and he had a nice look about him; a helplessness like he didn't have it in him to hurt anyone even if he did sometimes threaten to stab Angela with a kitchen knife. Mum knew he wasn't right in the head but she never showed concern; she never expressed fear of me being chopped up into little pieces by this mad drunken Irishman. The only danger was in believing the fantastic tales he told.

I'm watching The Benny Hill Show while he hunts around for a pair of socks. He opens a can of lager.

'Doo yer pleh guitar Rhob?' He asks.

I shrug, 'No.'

'I used tae, I maete do a few numbers in my maates band tonayyyte.'

I didn't know Pat was in a band, 'Oh are you a singer Pat?'

'What?? I've bin in loads of bands, have you ever heard of Hoat Chocolate?' and with that, he picks up some 45's and selects 'Emily' by 'Hot Chocolate' and puts it on. Next minute as the song starts, he's up on his feet saying, 'I bloody wrote this song for them.'

Suddenly he's singing:

'We were together since we were five

She was so pretty.

Emma was a star in everyone's eyes.

And when she said she'd be a movie queen, nobody laughed.

Her face like an angel, she could be anything. Emmaline

Emma Emaline

I'm gonna write your name high on that silver screen.'

He's now picked up Glen's toy guitar. It's broken and has missing strings but Pat isn't aware and doesn't care; he holds it as if were his beloved Fender Stratocaster and with a look of pained emotion he strikes the strings in unison with the record screaming out, 'Emilin, da-da, da-da-da' OH Emiline, da-da da-da-da.' The guitar sounds like a band of discordant banjo frogs and I sit there with a polite smile on my face, not believing that babysitting could be this much fun. He goes on to tell me stories of when he was with Hot Chocolate and how he played with them and wrote songs with them and I'm sitting there nodding my head in mute amazement.

On a different babysitting venture, Pat tells me how he used to be a tournament chess player and played against Russia. He gets out a chessboard and teaches me the chess moves. I'd never bothered before with chess. I was more a draughts kind of guy. Chess looked too complicated but Pat was patient and I found it to be easier than I thought it'd be. I later taught Debbie how to play and we added it to our reservoir of things to do when it was miserable outside, all courtesy of Pat.

    My mate Tris has come to babysit with me. He doesn't believe my 'Pat' stories but Pat is in top form and gives us an hour of unbelievable entertainment. He tells us how he used to hang around with The Beatles and helped write some of their songs. Out comes the broken guitar and on go The Beatles records as he sings to song after song, twanging his discordant chords while he twists his hips, 'Hey Jude, don't let us down.' He plays as if performing on stage to ten thousand people, hardly aware of me and Tris sitting there enjoying the show.

CHAPTER 27 — Pat and The Cop Shop

Pat's relationship with Angela doesn't last and their separation is long and full of drama with many drunken episodes of Pat wandering around Chulsa Estate with his kitchen knife. But then he melts away out of our lives. I bump into him many years later in my mid-twenties but under the circumstances of that situation, I don't acknowledge him, nor does he me.

I was in a relationship with Sarah at the time and we had a daughter, Natalie. We lived in the Lambeth area near Waterloo Bridge in a top floor two-bed Peabody Housing Association flat.

We had been out all day over at Hyde Park picnicking with a friend of ours, Jenny and Sarah's stepfather, Tom. Jenny was a hairdresser like me and we worked together at Mates Hair Studio in Sydenham. We were great buddies and had a thing for each other but had never acted on it. Well not then and anyway, I loved Sarah, even though she had lost interest in me.

We all lay there on the grass in the soft afternoon sun drinking wine and chatting about life while Natalie gathered daisies and buttercups. Tom charmed us with his humour and the company was good for Sarah and me; we needed the distraction. But when we got home, we had a massive argument about what, I can't remember and then Sarah's brother Paul came around and began abusing Sarah about something. Well, I was in a bad mood and didn't want him going off his head in my house and I wanted to be a hero, so I threw him out.

That changed the flow of the river. Sarah and I made up and entered that summer evening in an easier mood.

Back in those days I smoked marijuana and had a couple of my own plants standing on the kitchen windowsill. I was very proud of my cultivation and would often pick off a few leaves, dry them in the oven and roll my own. So, as the warm evening drew in, Sarah and Tom, who had come around, sat drinking beer, while I smoked my homegrown.

Sarah's brother, Paul, was an unusual person. He'd never held a job down for long and was now in his late twenties. Doctors discovered when he was thirteen, he had schizophrenia, so his mother tried to protect and shelter him. This resulted in an overindulged and spoiled person and he knew how to keep the flow of money coming from his mother's purse. He was close to Sarah and I and she often supported him when he was on a downer but sometimes he could turn nasty. What I didn't realise, as I sat in my flat smoking, was Paul felt very nasty about me and had gone to the first pay phone he could find to call the police.

'Hello Lambeth Police Station, please state the reason for your call.'

'There's a stash of drugs and marijuana plants at York House, Hercules Road, Waterloo. The guy that lives there is a dope dealer.'

So, as I sat on my couch, chilling with a joint in my mouth, two policemen were stalking outside our flat, peering into the kitchen window, admiring my marijuana plants and waiting to make their move. A knock on the door and in they came.

It's a shocking sight to be confronted with dark blue official uniforms in one's home. I guessed I was in trouble but managed with unbelievable speed to put my joint out in the ashtray and slide it under the couch.

From the tip-off they received, they expected and hoped I would be a good catch; a drug lord right under their nose. When they saw I only had two plants, which were obviously for my use, one policeman apologised, 'Look, I'm sorry, this isn't something that would interest us but as we've acted on the call, we have to charge you.'

They took me and my plants and charged me. From the time they charged me, through to my court appearance, I got to know one of the policemen well. He told me, 'You're the nicest guy I've ever arrested, I'd much rather arrest you than anyone else!' I thought that was funny. I was fined fifteen pounds.

On the night they charged me, I confess I was worried. I didn't know if I was in big trouble or not. Some cops were hard-nosed and questioned me hard, trying to determine who and what I was. I didn't see myself as a criminal and despite my situation, I wanted to be considered an upstanding member of the community, who just happened to enjoy marijuana.

Then they brought another guy in; some drunk who had probably been disturbing the peace. The way he swayed; I didn't believe he could have been guilty of much more. Looking closer, I recognised him. It was Pat. I hadn't seen him for many years but there was no mistaking him. Pat was a lovely guy and a harmless person but trouble followed him wherever he went. If the cops saw I knew Pat, they wouldn't think I was as well adjusted, as I was trying to portray. If they saw me on close terms with this drunken Irishman, there's no telling how that may have changed their impression of me. He looked at me for a moment but didn't appear to recognise me. To my shame, I stood there not saying anything. Then they marched us off to separate desks to have glowing reports written about us.

That's the last I saw of Pat. I wish I'd spoken to him; I'm sorry I didn't go over to him and give him a big smile. I wonder where he is today, if he's still alive? He could well be living in a doss house somewhere; a very broken and lonely individual. But I believe in God and I trust God has something good in store for him. One day.

CHAPTER 28 — Nola

Mum and Angela are close friends but Mum is also close to Nola Robbins who lives upstairs. My first recollection of Nola is when Mum takes me and Deb down to Well's Park for a picnic by the paddling pools. We love these picnics; Mum makes a few rounds of egg and tomato sandwiches and a big bottle of orange squash, chucks it all in a bag with a few bags of crisps and off we go.

It was a lovely Saturday early afternoon and Mum threw a big blanket on the ground a few metres up from the paddling pools. There were three paddling pools joined together on different levels, starting with the smallest at the top end which attracted the smallest kids. That pool flowed into a larger pool, which itself flowed into an even larger pool lower down which attracted the bigger kids. There was also a little cabin kiosk where we'd buy ice lollies and there was a putting green; it's all gone now with only a slight hint of what once was.

Nola arrived with her two little boys Jarrad and Jerry and they joined us. Nola was a gentle lady, a little on the shy side but lovely and gentle. She had longish light brown hair, pulled back into a ponytail, a slightly prominent nose and big soft blue eyes with small pupils. she reminded me of a bird, not the predaceous type, there was nothing predatory about Nola. With her sensitivity, timidity and alertness, she reminded me more of the prey. But she wasn't nervous or jumpy; in fact, she had a lovely softness about her. She seemed so innocent and pretty. Her husband Burt was a big tall man, also gentle and full of good cheer. As I hit my teens, I babysat for them when they went out. She was probably in her mid-twenties when we first met.

Like Angela, she often came and sat with Mum, chatting

over coffee; she and her kids became a part of our lives.

Early one morning someone was knocking on our door. I was half asleep and let it go but Mum answered it, 'Nola?' I hear a commotion and Mum screaming and Nola shouting obscenities. I don't know what happened next but Nola had attacked Mum and then ran off.

It turned out that poor Nola had schizophrenia. That beautiful, lovely young lady; a mother and wife, had a disease I would hear a lot about over the years.

We learned how to manage Nola to a degree. We knew when to open the door and let her in and we knew when to not answer, hoping she'd go away. When she changed, she would try to seek Mum out but Mum wasn't so keen to be found on days like those.

Unfortunately, and tragically, Nola's mental health issues became worse and had a disastrous effect on their family life. Nola and Burt eventually split up and Nola spent occasional time in Cane Hill mental hospital. Occasionally she escaped, once with another lady and they both came and descended on Mum and drank tea with her all afternoon. Poor Mum, sitting there uncomfortably in her chair, petrified, trying to make polite conversation and all the time wondering whether she might at any moment and without warning be set upon.

The Robbins family move to Wales and Nola will eventually die of complications, probably brought on from years of strong medication. Nola's youngest boy is in the UK somewhere. As for Jarrad, Nola's oldest boy, he will move to Australia and will be happily married with children. He's gonna be a big guy, untidy, with a cheerful loppy smile. He'll need a bit of mothering and he will have a lovely wife who will look after him.

CHAPTER 29 — Audrey

We have some unusual friends but the oddest of all is Audrey Sharn. She lives upstairs; the same flat the Goods will move into. She's the first friend, if we could call her that, Mum's ever had on the estate.

My first encounter with her was one Saturday lunchtime when Deb and I were coming home from the shops. Mum was working at her sister's cafe in Herne Hill; Deb and I had gone up to Crystal Palace to spend our pocket money. It had been raining sporadically all morning but then the heavens opened wider, cleaning the streets of all people. We took refuge in a wet café; the windows steamed up and streaming with condensation. Everywhere were wet coats and dripping umbrellas as the café packed with people like us, escaping from the heavy rain, all sitting around with our hot cups of tea and elevenses; warm air rising from the plates into the atmosphere. It felt like it was raining in there too.

We caught the 227-bus home from the Crystal Palace Parade where all the buses alight. The 227 still runs today and I feel a warm glow every time I see that bus coming along the road. I've been catching it since I was six years old, to my infant school and then junior school before graduating to the senior school, not to mention for the many other reasons to go up and down the hill.

The 227 bus is a part of my history, it's as big a part of my past as is the Crystal Palace Park. Goodness, I even got run over once and ended up in the hospital for two weeks from trying to catch that bus.

The design of the 227 bus has changed over the years but it's still red and still single decked but it wouldn't do any good to fish around in one's pocket for the fare today; everybody uses an Oyster charge card. Trying to use money today would be like someone in my day trying to pay the fare with gold pieces.

Seeing the 227-bus service is still in operation makes me believe life can still be simple like it should be, like village life on 'Postman Pat;' always the same. Maybe when I'm old and delirious and won't co-operate with the ward nurses, all I'll need to be settled down is for someone to write the number 227 or simply say, 'Don't worry Rob, the bus is coming, it's a 227, are you getting on?' I reckon that'll be as good as any medication.

It was only a short journey from Crystal Palace to home, three short stops. We would have walked and spent the bus fare on sweets but we were soaked and wanted to be home in the dry and warm.

By the time we got back home, it was bucketing down even heavier, with gusts of wind blowing us around. We were struggling, making our way along the road towards our house. I noticed a lady standing outside on her balcony window on the third-floor shouting at us.

'What are you doing in the rain?'

She seemed alarmed and so, with her bidding, we took the lift to her house. A gingery red-headed lady opened the door and ushered us in saying, 'You poor little devils what are you doing out there, you're soaked.'

She asked us lots of questions as she dried us off and fed us with hot soup 'Where are your parents?' 'Where's your mum?' 'Where does she work?' 'Where've you been?' 'Where's your dad?' 'What happened to your dad?' 'Who's looking after you?' 'When does your mum get home?'

She eventually let us go after we told her everything and when Mum came home, Audrey came down and bullied her way into our lives.

She became friends with Mum and together they arranged for me to go up to her house the following Saturday so Audrey could keep an eye on me and Deb while Mum was at work. But where was Debbie? It appears she didn't have to go up to Audrey's. But I had to. Audrey asked the usual barrage of questions, sat me down and asked me if I could play cards.

'Yes.'

'What can you play?'

'I can play Rummy.'

'Oh, can you teach me?'

'Yes ok.'

We sat there by the French windows looking down over the estate and played cards while the noises of my friends outside playing wafted up to us. I didn't want to sit there teaching an older lady how to play a card game. Hopefully it wouldn't take long; Rummy was an easy game to learn. The object of the game was to create two good hands; a pair, a triple, a run or a house. Each player discarded a useless card and picked up another one until the player was ready to call and then the best hand won. She picked it up but I won. 'OK I'll deal now.' She said

It seemed I had to play more than one game. I tried not to show my disappointment but I was constantly looking out of the window. What baffles me is why she would want to have me sitting with her playing cards. Where were her two little kids? And where was her husband? What was she doing playing card games in an empty house with an 11-year-old boy?

I sat there hoping that each game of Rummy would be the last but then she'd say, 'OK Your turn to deal' and then we'd be off again.

After what seemed to be a dozen games she said, 'OK I guess you want to go off and play do you?'

I nodded and took off as fast as I could.

She was a strange lady; negative, heavy and harsh but under that she was like the rest of us, needing love and acceptance. Her husband, Ed worked for ITV and seemed a very nice quiet man and kind. Her two little children, both with deep red hair were beautiful but Audrey seemed uninterested in them; I think her daughter feared her. Audrey seemed uninterested in her husband Ed too. Her little boy wore callipers, I don't know what had happened there.

One day she took me on a trip to Brighton with them for the day. I loved Brighton, it was London's nearest seaside and I was very excited to be going. I imagined all the things we'd be doing; playing on the beach, swimming in the ocean, going on the funfair rides, spending money on the amusements and in the arcades, eating candy floss and toffee apples, I could hardly wait. It was Audrey, her husband Ted, their two children and another family. We travelled down by coach and when we arrived, we plonked ourselves on the stony beach by some ugly huge concrete support structure. And there we stayed the whole day while the adults got the sun on their faces.

Audrey didn't want me to walk down to the beach; she wasn't confident about letting me go too far away despite my protest that I could swim. They also weren't interested in going to the funfair, nor the arcades, nor any of the amusements. They weren't interested in candy floss nor toffee apples. The most exciting thing I did that was to walk about twenty-five yards away to a kiosk to buy a Mars Bar. When I came back, Audrey wanted to know what I was eating, where I bought it, how much it cost me, where did I get the money from, did my mum allow me to buy my own sweets and not to go too far away. So, I sat there in the baking sun for the next several hours. We had sandwiches in the afternoon and a glass of orange squash. I was relieved when we left.

Often when Audrey was in our house, she'd say she could feel a bad presence there and that we might have ghosts and she often said negative things, she knew how to darken the atmosphere. I'm sure it was her who called the Social Security to do a check on Mum telling them she had a part-time job that was undeclared. They came to check on us and Mum had to pack her job in which meant we had less money to live on.

One-night Mum hit the wall and had a meltdown. Wouldn't you know it, Audrey was right there. Seeing Mum in despair and losing the plot reminded me of her suicidal stuff from our past. I started crying, Audrey reached forward, grabbed me by the shoulders saying, 'there there,' and she pulled me right up tight towards her and brought my face slap bang right deep into her breasts which were cold and clammy; I felt like I needed to wipe my face with a towel afterward.

One night when Audrey was at our house, she told Mum she knew how to hypnotise people. For some unknown reason, Mum allowed her to hypnotise Debbie, who was all of six years old. Debbie drifted around the house for the rest of the night like a half-asleep zombie, doing everything Mum told her, she even went to bed when asked, without question. It wasn't until years later that she admitted she had been hoaxing the whole time.

Debbie was such an actor and I bet she was acting the time I knocked her out in the living room. It was something I'd learned at school in the playground. The idea was to get someone to do lots of press-ups and touching toes until out of breath, then get them to take a deep breath and hold it while you give them a bear hug and squeeze the life out of them, the result being that everything goes fuzzy, dizziness sets in and you feel you might faint. We were so excited to discover this new game at school and we were all doing it to each other.

One evening I decided I'd try it out on my sister. Mum was watching TV or reading a book. Debbie and I were playing together at the other end of the lounge when I remembered my trick and asked Deb if I could try it on her. She was as willing as hell to try it but wanted it to work so I made her do more push-ups and touching toes until she was out of breath, then I made her take a huge deep breath and when she held it, I stepped behind her, picked her up into a bear hug and squeezed the living daylights out of her and didn't stop. Then she became heavy and slumped forward. She became so heavy and I dropped her and she hit her head on the brown tiled floor, which made quite a loud noise, 'thump.'

I panicked thinking I'd killed her and looked to see if Mum noticed. Mum had heard the thump looked over to see Debbie's cold still body on the floor. Mum shrieked 'What's happened?, What have you done?'

'Nothing,' I blurted, 'It was an accident'

She came rushing over as I tried to explain that it was just a game, something I picked up from the school playground. Debbie stirred back into consciousness but she wasn't herself the whole night. I think I really did knock her out.

I don't know what happened to the Sharns. One day they moved away. I wondered what their children would grow into; they seemed to have their father's soft nature but their mother's influence?

The daughter will visit Mum many years later. Mum will remark on what a lovely looking girl she is, with beautiful red hair and a lovely nature.

CHAPTER 30 — Mums and Stereos

Out of all my mates' mothers, I reckon my mum is the prettiest, although it's unanimous among my mates and me that Deirdre's mum Penny is the schoolboy's choice. She's tall with tinted fair hair, lifted and loose and she lengthens her height with slow graceful movements; like a Negress; a white Negress, as if she's balancing a water bowl on her head. There's not one boy among us who doesn't share a secret desire of wanting to be alone with her; being told to close the bedroom door and draw the curtains.

I fantasised about being in that special place in time and space, where everything familiar and normal disappears and the hidden emerges, curious and alluring - only for the eyes of the chosen few; the special. She evoked these feelings and thoughts in many of us, which we shared with each other and she would talk to us slowly and deliberately, holding our gazes in her open, half smile. I wondered whether she knew about our boyhood cravings.

Tris' Mum was different, she made the best egg and chips in the world and was the ideal mum. She always looked at Tris as if he'd done something wrong but it was a scowl masking undying love. A mere suggestion of hunger from her boy had her cracking eggs and getting the chips into the pan. And anytime I was around, I'd join in too; fried eggs, beans and chips with a big splat of tomato sauce and several slices of white buttered bread, yum!

My mate Blake Coates, 'Badger,' his mum gave the best beltings; he took some big hidings from her just about every other week for something or other; right in front of us too. But they were a loving, gregarious family and always welcomed me and Tris with open arms at their house and we loved being there.

Paul Winston's Mum was the hardest worker, raising six children without a husband and unlike my family, I don't think she claimed social security. I imagine the elder boys helped financially; they worked together out of necessity.

Some mums were hard looking and had given up trying to look attractive years ago but my mum still liked making herself look pretty. She had her feminine role models, various movie stars and singers but the person she modelled herself on most was Petula Clark. I didn't realise just how much until I saw Petula Clark perform at The Mundaring Weir Hotel here in Western Australia in 2011.

Seeing Petula on stage, her hand movements and the way she danced around was just like watching Mum. I hadn't realised until then how much of an influence this English star had been on Mum. We had bundles of her records and Shirley Bassey, Frankie Lane, all the Burt Bacharach songs, Dusty Springfield, Nelson Eddy, Gene Pitney and much more. Music was a huge thing in our house.

One day Mum told me and Deb there was a new thing called 'stereo.' 'Imagine,' she said, 'hearing the drums in one corner of the living room and the guitars in the other corner and the singing voice in the centre. That's stereo, it's just like having the group playing in the living room.'

This sounded amazing and Mum had put a deposit down on a stereo radiogram. It didn't matter we paid too much money for it or that the interest was too high and Mum would have this debt hanging over her head for three years. We couldn't wait.

The day came when our radiogram arrived and we placed it against the living room wall. We all sat there staring at it like a newly discovered relative. If Mum had said go and put the kettle on, it'll be thirsty; me and Deb would have been into that kitchen like lightning.

The time came for it to play us a song. I put an album over the centre spindle and pulled the plastic bar over onto it, then I pulled the 'auto' switch that set the motion. The LP dropped onto the spinning turntable and then with an awkward robotic movement the arm swung, first back and then forward into position and then dropped slowly onto the LP. As the stylus touched down onto the vinyl, there was the muffled crackling sound of the amplifier picking up the sound of friction, that momentary pause before the music begins.

When the music began, I waited for the stereo effect to give me that 'wow' sensation. But you know what? It didn't. It was nice hearing the music coming out of two different speakers, even if they were only one metre apart from one another but I wasn't getting the true stereo effect. The guitar, drums and voice weren't being projected to different parts of the room; just an equal amount of musical distribution from each speaker. Still, we had prepared ourselves to be excited and we couldn't let ourselves down. So, we all sat there and said, 'Wow it's fantastic!'

Over the years we played that radiogram till it could hardly stand up anymore. We loved it and worked it into the ground till it was too old to play and just wanted to be left alone. When records got scratched, we'd put coins on the stylus to weigh it down and force it into re-grooving the scratched bit, to stop that part of the song repeating itself over and over. If that didn't work, we'd weigh it down with more coins, so it was almost cutting through the record. We'd try to put six albums on the stack instead of three and by the time the sixth album was playing it wouldn't play properly and music would slur and spin. It was a tough life for a radiogram in the Craggs household; it did well to survive as long as it did.

We played records a lot and even though I was attracted to new groups like T. Rex, Slade and Gary Glitter, Debbie and I still enjoyed whatever Mum listened to.

One day Mum told me that Peter was out of prison and was coming to visit us.

'Robitt, Peter's out of prison.'

'Is he?'

'Yes, and he's coming to visit us tonight. Here's two pounds, do you want to go to the shops and buy some records?'

It seemed a normal enough request but I wonder about the thought process going on in Mum's head; 'Oh my goodness we have a visitor coming and we don't have enough records in the cupboard. What will we do? We can't play the same record all evening, what will people think? We'll know the words backward. We won't get the tune out of our heads for days. 'We can't have people thinking we're musically destitute.'

I asked Mum what records should I get?

'Anything; you choose something nice.'

I was pleased to be trusted with the important mission. I took the 227 bus straight up to Crystal Palace and picked out two shops; Woolworths and a nearby record shop.

It took hours to decide; I didn't have enough money to be experimental in my decision making, I had to be practical and after much soul searching settled on 'The Best Of Glen Miller' and an album called 'Rock Revival' with tracks like,

'Blueberry Hill' and 'Tequila.'

I had done well and we loved them. Peter was coming late, so poor Debbie was in bed. Mum was knocking her sherry back like orange juice. In later years she swapped the wine glass for a coffee mug. That's still her style today, God bless her.

Autumn had arrived, it wasn't cold but it was getting darker earlier in the evenings. There was something cosy about having the living room lit up with side lamps and the whole evening still ahead.

There was a knock at the door. Mum sent me to answer. I felt like her butler. 'Yes sir, Mrs Blake is at home and she will see you, please step this way.'

I knew Peter wasn't coming back to live with us again and I was glad about that but I was excited and very curious to see him.

I opened the door and didn't recognise the man standing there. Before me was a slim man wearing glasses and dressed in a suit and tie. If he'd told me he was Buddy Holly and he was selling insurance, I'd have believed him.

'i i is V Vera Craggs at home please?'

He appeared not to recognise me and he sounded so official!

'Yeah, she's in there.' I stood there gaping at him.

'Ca ca can you tell her, P Peter B Blake is here to sssee her?'

'Yeah, she said you're to come in.'

Prison life had served him well, he looked like a new

man; polite and smart looking too. Prison couldn't be that bad, I thought.

Mum let me stay up for a couple of hours; I don't think she wanted to be alone with Peter. I don't know what they talked about; all that adult talk went over my head. Then Mum told me to put the records on.

Earlier in the day, I had been practising dancing to the rock 'n' roll songs with a balloon. My idea was to kick the balloon against the sitting room wall and re-kick it on the rebound. It was my own invention, soccer-balloon-squash to rock-n-roll music. Because the balloon was light and stayed in the air for a long time, I was able to get some quirky dance moves in before kicking the balloon again. Mum said I was good at it.

'Shall I show Peter when he comes tonight?' I asked

'Yes, I'm sure he'll love to see it.' She smiled.

I can't help thinking how naïve I was for a twelve-year-old. I think of me and Deb as both being very naïve for our ages.

They sat there, drinking sherry and beer and talked about things, skirted around some other things and totally avoided other things. Mum would often turn the conversation towards me whenever she felt herself in a tight situation and they'd both smile at me and say something nice. I think Mum was relieved when I asked if Peter wanted to see my football dance.

I think the song was Tequila and I hammered into the balloon and did the best tricks I could conjure up, glancing occasionally over my shoulder to see how impressed they were with my skilful moves.

Da-da dada da-da dada, da-da dada da dada Te-qui-la!! I rocked and rolled and bounced that balloon up against the wall, looking back at them for their enthusiastic charming smiles and encouragement.

After a short while Peter's smile was wearing off and he was looking a lot less like Buddy Holly and a lot more like an insurance salesman. They were both sitting there smiling at me. They had reached an impasse and didn't know what to do or how to do it.

Mum was doing a much better job of keeping her smile on though. She was sitting on the edge of the couch perched on the edge all-polite like, as if she was entertaining guests at a posh hotel. Her hair was all done and nice, her fine hair back combed into thick bounces. Her eyes were moist and glassy and she looked lovely in that dimly lit room; so very attractive, so very unsure.

I gave them another round of balloon soccer against the wall to 'Let's Dance' and Mum then drew my entertainment to an end and sent me to bed. Then Peter could tell Mum how much he loved her, how he missed her, how he had changed for the better and how Deb and I needed a father. I don't know that's what he said. But it would make sense. Anyway, Mum never had him back, even if she had thought about it. But he became a part of our lives again.

He moved into a bedsit up at Crystal Palace and they decided he would see Debbie on Saturdays and I would go along too. He would be in the Crystal Palace Hotel drinking with his mates and we'd meet him up there about twelve-thirty. I'd pop my head in and let him know we were there. He would be in a superb mood with a healthy measure of beer-swilling around inside him. He wasn't wearing his suit any longer and his glasses were gone.

'I'm gonna be about another ten minutes ok? Wanna coke, packet of crisps? I won't be long; you don't mind do you?'

Within five minutes, he'd return with Coke and crisps for us and we'd sit munching and drinking our treats at a garden table in the pub car park. We'd scored. This would go on for about thirty minutes with more crisps more coke and Peter getting into an even cheerier mood, then he'd eventually pry himself away from his mates at the bar.

What do you want to do? Shall we go uptown? How about Buckingham Palace? Are you hungry?

Yes yes yes yes! It was all a treat to us: buses, tubes, burgers, chips, eating, drinking, feeding the pigeons, Trafalgar Square, museums. We'd come home with cheap souvenirs and stories of our day and Mum would listen with a big smile on her face while getting tea ready. Sometimes, if Peter brought us home, he'd try to talk Mum into going out in the evening for a drink. She'd go if she was in the right mood. Sometimes, he'd give me and Deb a pound each and tell us to go down to the shops to buy ourselves some chocolates and to take our time. That was an offer we'd never refuse. We were easily played.

We went out most Saturdays; Peter was trying to make a good impression and to be fair, he kept up a good steady contact with Debbie for many years. Once when I wasn't there, Debbie was on the bus on the top deck with Peter and she had a little mini fit. Peter hollered at everyone to shut the fuck up! I'm glad he did that for her and I bet Deb felt good when she saw her dad acting out for her.

But our dads aren't there for us. In Peter's case, he's not even there for himself; he never takes care of himself. Socks remain on his feet for weeks. Even his bedsit looks forlorn. Bereft of company and neglected, it's left to take care of itself; it's a place to sleep, maybe read a book or the paper and then out, door shut, windows closed, stale air trapped with nowhere to go. Peter has an excuse, if he can't even take care of himself, how can he take care of us?. I'm not sure *my* dad has an excuse.

CHAPTER 31 — Kentwood Senior

September has arrived and I'm now attending Kentwood Senior High School, which for the first few months is at its old site in Penge near my junior school in Oakfield Road. We'll soon be moved to the new site in Beckenham. I'm expecting good things at Kentwood, having risen to the top at Malcolm Junior School where life has been good and I look forward to all that Kentwood promises. The school uniform is smart and I can't wait to wear it; dark grey flannel trousers, dark charcoal blazer with a gold and green griffin sewn on the front breast pocket, white shirt and a green and blue diagonal striped tie. Kentwood here I come!

I was in for a shock. Malcolm Junior School was a small safe womb compared to the noisy and rough Kentwood. I missed having girls around; I was brought up in an all-female household; no dad; no male influence. Perhaps if I'd been rougher around the edges, I wouldn't have missed Malcolm's modern, clean and warm environment; it wouldn't have bothered me that Kentwood was beaten through; cold and archaic.

I pretended the stern teachers who always yelled, didn't faze me and I ignored the bigger kids who sneered at us but I felt off balance there and insecure.

Things improved when we moved to Beckenham; the environment being much better with big green playing fields and nicer buildings; much less intimidating and depressing like the previous school. Still, I witnessed a knife fight on my first day there between Pete Brothers and Bob Johnson.

A big circle of us stood around them nearby the school gate. The hard-grey tarmac ground as cold as the November day. As they circled each other, each with their knives in hand, I noticed Bob's brother, Ed, on the edge of the ring edging Bob onward, 'Cut him, Bob, go on stick him!' Pete Brothers looked around, bewildered, sussed up the situation, then turned and ran, breaking through the circle, taking off with shouts and catcalls of humiliation following him. I reckon he made the right decision.

This was a scary and exciting start to senior school life; I wondered how I would get through the next four years. It didn't take too long before I ran into my first big problem and with a Johnson. It was the following year after the influx of the new year one's into the school.

It was raining and that meant no games, so we had to sit in the assembly hall. I didn't mind as I'd forgotten to bring my games kit and no kit meant getting the slipper – a hard whack across the backside with a trainer. No games meant no worries about needing our kit. Nevertheless, Mr Heart, the games teacher, got up onto the stage and made every boy stand up and show him their kit. If they didn't have it, they were brought up onto the stage and slippered in front of the assembly.

Many of us, including me, got the slipper. Mr Heart almost overlooked Melvyn Peel but we, his best mates, could not allow our good friend to get away with something like that. Poor Melvyn, both hands rubbing his backside like it was on fire.

Mr Heart, having satiated himself on our misfortunes headed off for his lunch, leaving us with our red backsides. We splintered off into smaller groups, telling jokes and stories, laughing and swearing at each other. After a while, the hall became quiet as kids went out to play. I sat there swapping football cards with someone when a boy sitting in front turned and snatched a card right out of my hand.

'Oy give it back,' I yelled

'What'ya gonna do about it?' He snarled at me.

I realised he was Paul Johnson; his brothers had a notorious reputation and I was too scared to get into a tangle with him so I backed down and forgot all about it. But he didn't and he had every intention of exploiting my fear, as I soon discovered.

A few weeks later at the end of the school day, I was walking toward the bus stop with a friend. It was a cold autumn day and I was wearing my duffel coat.

'Oy mate,' a kid was calling from behind, 'He just spat on your back.'

He pointed at Paul Johnson who was walking behind me, chewing gum and looking very cocky; he didn't deny it. I took my coat off to check it and sure enough, there was a big white foamy gob of spit on the back. I have to say, I was scared, I'd already backed away from this person once before and he had mockery all over his face. So, I had no choice; I'd lose a lot if I walked away, I faced up to him and got the first punch in with a right-hand side hook which caught the left side of his chin. I backed away to avoid being punched back.

He looked furious. I went to go for him again but as I did he blurted out, 'All right, you already got me once.'

I could hardly believe what he'd said. He didn't want anymore. I turned away relieved and elated. I wondered whether he might send his brothers to come and dismantle me but I also hoped he'd be too scared to let them know he'd backed down. Maybe they'd give him a hiding for his cowardice.

I had many fights at Kentwood and experienced the glory of victory and the pain of humiliating defeat. Cowardice too, like the time when Mick Conner tried to get money off me. I wouldn't give him any, so he slugged me with a side hook and I was too scared to hit him back; something I regret.

I've often wondered how fantastic it would be to have the chance to re-live that moment with Mick again. Might I react the same way? Problem is, I'd still be the same person in the same situation. I'd prefer to replay it, not as I was then but as I am now; with older and more experienced eyes. Yes, that's a fantasy. We can't go through all our previously lived lives tidying it up like a parent cleaning up after a messy child. But the thought process led me to write a short fantasy story, which I've inserted into this memoir:

THE SECONDER

My name is Bob and I've just turned 45; for the second time. I'm a Seconder. In case you don't know what that is; it means I'm reliving my life a second time around. I started Seconding thirty-two years ago when I first became 45. One minute I was 45 and the next minute I was thirteen. And now I've reached 45 again. I guess that makes me 77 if you do the numbers. That's how long I've been alive. You can tell but you have to be very observant.

I tried to keep it a secret because at worst, Seconders are vulnerable; gangsters kidnap and torture us for future information and at the very least, people just don't understand us. They envy the opportunities we have. I understand where they're coming from. When I was a first timer I often dreamed of getting a second chance at life. I fantasised how easy it would be to become a millionaire and patch up all the mistakes made first time around. But it doesn't work like that. It's very hard trying to remember your past when it's still ahead of you. I remember waiting for one incident to happen again so I could change it for the better. It never came. Some things did re-happen but mostly with changes. I tell you; it can really mess up your mind.

How did I become a Seconder? Everyone's story is different. With me, it happened after a period of counselling sessions. With the help of my good counsellor, I discovered how very powerful the past is. It was a shocking realisation to see how the past co-exists with the present. It reminds me of an experience I once had as a young man.

I was on an LSD trip and I noticed a corkscrew lying on the coffee table. Just an ordinary metal corkscrew with those side levers and the middle part designed as a bottle top remover. You know, it looks like a metal person. I sat there staring at it for a while and I began to realise this was something I'd never seen before in my entire life; I was seeing it for the first time. Corkscrews have always been around but I'd not taken notice before; I was, becoming more and more awed by the beauty of its existence as each moment passed by. I was in a state of shocking wonder.

That's how my past hit me. I discovered its reality; its present existence, its overwhelming influence. My discovery of the power of the past hit me as hard as that corkscrew. The only difference, I always smile whenever I see a corkscrew. They look so friendly. As for my past, well; I'm learning to embrace it. It's always been here with me; overseeing everything I do.

I was pondering this one night as I soaked in the bath and as I followed my thoughts, I found myself in my mind's eye being carried to a dimly lit corridor. It was the corridor outside my French class in my old senior school and Mick stood there; he had me backed up against a corridor wall and was trying to bully me into lending him some money; money I'd never see again for sure. I told him I had none and I knew what was coming next.

But this memory was different. First, it felt more real than a memory and second, I felt like I, Bob, the forty-five-year-old man was in Robert the thirteen-year-old boy. It was me, Bob the older, witnessing this past event. It didn't occur to me I had started Seconding.

The punch came on the side of the face. Damn, I felt it! Was this real? Fear swept over me; I looked down to see if I was still in the bath. I wasn't. I looked back up, straight into eyes of Mick O'Connor; the smell of his unwashed hair and 'Brut' aftershave in the air. The same aftershave we all wore. I didn't like this aroma emanating from him; such a lovely scent, such an ugly bastard.

He was wearing his Harrington jacket, ripped and old. His Levi jeans shiny with dirt and cut short in the legs. His brown Dr. Martens boots unpolished with a hole cut in the front toecap to show off the steel underneath.

The punch didn't hurt. It was more a shock; my original fear back then had been that he might hit me again but he hadn't; and then he started to walk away with his sloppy grin. The thought came that I had always wanted to punch him back. I was still scared but I spoke without thinking. 'Mick.'

He turned to me in surprise.

'Good punch Mick,' I said this giving him a big smile, though my heart was pumping.

'What d'you say?'

'You have a good punch Mick, well done.'

He walked up to me. Close. 'D'you want more'

His nose was almost touching mine and he was looking for fear on my face. 'D'you hear wot I said?'

I smiled back at him. 'Oh yes please Mick, I want you to break my fucking nose.'

He let the smile drop from his face to show me I was in big trouble with him. I knew this tactic. He was getting ready to hit me again but he was holding back. This gave me confidence.

'BOO,' I yelled into his face and he jumped back off balance. 'That got ya, didn't it?'

He looked confused, even wary but he needed to salvage his respect. He came at me with an obvious side hook, which I blocked with my left arm. I counter struck with a forward straight punch, which caught his right eye. I stepped back to give myself space and kicked up into his groin, which brought him down to his knees. So far I had simply defended myself but I had to do more. I had to seriously hurt him. I did it more out of fear that if I didn't hurt him, he'd come back again once he had licked his wounds. So, I grabbed a handful of his hair and twisted it until he screamed. I told him I'd do worse to him if he ever came back at me again. He spat out his understanding with confusion written all over his face.

I knew by then I was Seconding but I was too hyped to consider the implications. I realised I was stuck and would be going through my whole life all over again. I needed to think. There was no book to explain how to handle Seconding. What was I supposed to do? I wandered down the corridor trying to get my thoughts together. A teacher stepped around the corner. It was Mr Whitaker, 'Craggs,' he shouted, 'shouldn't you be heading off to History?' Against my will, I fell straight into the pattern, 'Yes sir.'

'Well go on,' he said, 'off you go.'

So off I went, to History.

So, what was all that about? I'm not going to address the violence but do I have a desire to re-write my history?

Yes. There are parts of life where I wish I had acted more bravely or with more honour, parts where I would like to have treated people better than they deserved. It's a natural desire. But it's more important to realise and accept we are who we are because of our history. We can learn from our past and create a better future by what we do now. We need to cherish the present.

Anyway, I wasn't the only one to suffer at the hands of Mick O'Conner; he was always slugging someone in the face. A few years after I opened my hairdressing salon in Penge, an old schoolmate of mine, David Barter, came in for a haircut and while Dawn, my stylist cut his hair we told funny 'Mick' stories. His was by far the funniest I'd ever heard.

Dave was walking home from school when he bumped into Mick who was walking along Penge High Street with one of his mates, Paul Hedges. Mick calls Dave over and says, 'Give us a piggyback' and with that hops onto Dave's back and says to Paul, 'You hop on his back.' So, there's Dave and his mate with Mick and Paul on their backs and then Mick says, 'Ok, take me home' and with that Dave and his mate are taxiing Mick and Paul to their homes.

As Dave walked along the road with Mick on his back, he noticed a girl he fancied coming out of Woolworths. He didn't want to appear as someone's footstool so he tried to act casual as he slowed down to chat with her as if it was the most normal thing in the world to have someone on one's back.

'Where're you going?' She asked.

'Oh, I'm shooting up to Mick's house.'

It was obvious to her that Mick was using him as his own personal human taxi. Dave never got his girl.

The sad thing is that as an adult Mick developed schizophrenia. About a week after Dave had been in the salon, I was upstairs in my salon in the staff room having lunch when Dawn called, 'Rob, Mick's here to see you.'

I laughed, thinking she was joking and that it was probably Dave, so I came bounding downstairs and could hardly believe I was seeing Mick O'Conner standing right in front of me. I was shocked to see him, a bully from my past, standing in my salon. I didn't know why he was here or what he wanted but I didn't want him in my salon; didn't want him in my life. I believed that underneath his mental illness, he was still a nasty person and I knew I couldn't help him.

I decided to be bold and hit him with intimidating gregariousness. I walked right up close to him, grabbed his hand with mine, looked him close in the eyes with a big smile and said, 'Hi Mick, lovely to see you, how are you, what can I do for you?' The big bold approach worked. Whatever he'd been hoping to achieve didn't pan out. He fumbled, looking nervous being out of his territory and mumbled something like 'had I seen so and so.'

'No, I haven't seen him.'

Mick can't wait to get out of my salon and I'm relieved to see him go. I wonder what he wanted. Can't imagine it was to create a friendship. I wonder what his childhood was like. Did it cause his nastiness or was it his schizophrenia? So many bastards grew out of their bastardness but not him and in the end, I don't think he knew how to be any different. It's so hard to imagine him discovering love. But he will. He's as equal a child of this universe as me. Love will come his way.

CHAPTER 32 — Clubs, Cigarettes and Gangs

Paul Winston and I have become much better mates again, now we've started at Kentwood. He, like myself, is from a broken family but a large family with Paul being fourth from the top. Next is his sister Vanessa and she's followed by Sue, the youngest. His family seems a stronger unit than ours; I think it helps there are lots of brothers and sisters, even if that means lots of shoving, pushing and punching. Vanessa belts her little sister Sue over something trivial, Paul belts Vanessa for bullying her younger sister, then bigger brother Pat belts Paul for hitting a girl, though I think Pat has a soft spot for Vanessa.

Vanessa was a tomboy and wore the same clothes as the rest of us: Monkey boots, Harrington jacket and Levi's. I have to say I never considered she was female until a few minutes one night by the washing lines behind Hurst House: We were all running around playing when I bumped into her; we kissed and her lips, so soft, nothing like I expected. She was a soft discovery, a beautiful surprise. Tomboy, she might be but there's no fooling me, she's female! We're distracted by a call from the crowd to move on, never again to return to that place, the opportunity never again arising and neither of us pushing for it. We're back to being mates.

Vanessa was smart, the only one out of all of us who passed the eleven-plus. She went onto grammar school. She confided in me many years later that she struggled academically for a while but she obviously lifted her game; she stayed her course. I also remember years later when we all started work she was paid to watch and write reports about television shows. Fancy that, watching 'The Sweeney,' writing a few paragraphs about how good it was and receiving a cheque in the post for it.

Pat Winston, one of the older brothers was a big distant influence on us, like a faraway star with a gravitational pull; not that he allowed us to hang around with him until much later in life but he always told Paul what clothes to buy, what was in fashion and what was out and Paul shared this prized information with me. It was like we were spies and needed fashion intelligence. Pat wasn't our man in Havana, he was our man in Dales and all the other local men's fashion stores. Levi Jeans, loafers, Gibsons and Brogue shoes, Harrington Jackets, Crombie Coats, Brutus and Ben Sherman Shirts, Dr. Martens, Parka Jackets, Stay Press and Tonic trousers, towelling socks, bright coloured braces - without him to advise us, we bought nothing. Well, he'd tell Paul what and what not to buy and Paul would tell me.

But I bought a pair of Levi Jeans once before I knew better. I also bought a pair of loafers, all from Dales. I could have done with a big brother to help me out. Not having my informant meant I bought the wrong loafers and the wrong size jeans.

The news on the street was to buy the jeans one size larger than normal and hop into the bath until they shrunk to fit. So I hopped into the bath on Christmas Day wearing my oversized jeans and I was so excited. I sat in that bath till the water and I turned blue. After an hour, I got out of the bath like a wrinkled chip with my soaked jeans, which still felt somewhat massive. 'Well,' I thought, 'by the time they were dry they'd shrink more.' The next day was Boxing Day and I had them on and they fitted me like an oversized tent. They were still huge on me even three years later when I eventually wore them into the ground. I had to wear braces and a belt to keep them up. If I had a big brother, I doubt this would have happened. But I had learned. I wasn't going to buy a big pair of Levi's ever again.

As Paul and I hung around together, others gravitated into our orbit; there was Paul and his sister Vanessa, me, Tris Miles and his sister Jane, Rob Grant, Simon Lake and Pete Davidson aka Ripper. Others came and went and there are some whose names I've forgotten but Terry Goods, Richard Jefferson, Tim Belton, Dave Bacon, Badger and Steve Tracey – Tracer - all floated around our group.

We had discovered a social club called The Crypt, so called because it was down in the basement of a large Anglican church. Some Christians who wanted to help keep kids like us off the streets ran it. We thought they were an easy touch but they were smart; we were the dumb ones. We didn't realise they were doing this all for us, our egos only allowed for us to see ourselves as the most important people in the universe so there was no question of why they would put themselves out for us. Even the old greaser used to talk to them insolently. I don't remember his name but he looked like a biker and had tattoos and was a few years older than us. I thought he was going to be a lot of fun until the club leader told this greaser he needed someone strong and solid who could be relied on to help run the club and that was that. The greaser became the lap dog who wouldn't allow any cheek from us. He totally turned into one of them! How easily played he was. I could see it but I wasn't going to tell him that he had become their whipping boy. He'd whip me! But it was still a good club and only cost tuppence to get in.

We indulged in games and stood around trying to act cool listening to records with a cigarette in one hand and orange squash in the other. We hadn't long been smoking; I started off with menthol cigarettes as they were easier to inhale without coughing, then when I got used to them, I scrounged my mum's cigarette stubs out of her ashtray to roll my own.

The first time we smoked, I felt dizzy, then on a couple of occasions, a bit sick but I soon got used to the poison. It seemed it was a trial one had to go through to reach to the other side where the tried and tested, the best of the best resided; an illusion, we were driven by illusions.

We could only afford to buy single cigarettes from the sweet shop in Sydenham. They were a penny each; we knew we were being ripped off but we liked the shopkeeper, his nickname for me was Jo-Jo, which I liked. I think he was Turkish Cypriot, ever so jolly and friendly, happily serving all the customers, taking a penny here, a shilling there. He had no qualms serving us cigarettes and by selling them as singles, he was being proactive to market demands.

As a group, we were adopting our new identity. Not only were we smoking but we were developing an interest in clothes and we had all stopped having our hair cut, although my hair didn't grow down; more outward.

We also wore jewellery. We wore enough bangles on our wrists to make a Nigerian chief envious; then Tris and I became brave and walked down to the jeweller's in Sydenham to have our ears pierced with a sleeper and cross hanging off it. Only one ear though, the left ear; more than one or the right ear meant you were a queer.

So far though we hadn't yet established ourselves as a gang. We were simply kids hanging around together, playing football and wandering around the park and the streets.

Ripper had a big brother called Bob. Bob was a Neanderthal nutter. He and Kevin Crown made a scary duo. Sometimes they'd play soccer with us. We'd divide into two

Moving to Chulsa

teams, with Bob and Kevin always playing on the same side and woe to anyone who tackled them or dribbled the ball past them or even worse scored a goal against them; that would result in being chased and if caught, jumped on and pummelled to the ground. It paid to lose.

One of their delightful punishments was called The Knuckle. To 'knuckle' someone meant to clench the hand into a fist, then swipe the fist down across the top of the victim's head so that the edge of the knuckles would rap the head with a hard swipe. Ouch!

If they weren't trying to kick or knuckle us, they'd be shouting and hurling heinous insults at us but sometimes they'd grace us with their company. At times like this, we felt honoured to be near them.

It was Bob Davidson who told us we had to become a proper gang with a name and fight other gangs.

It's early evening; we're walking along the road at the bottom of the estate. Bob Davidson is across the road walking toward us. He crosses over the road.

'Watch ya, Bob,' we all say like a herd of sheep. We're like sheep but we think we're bulls!

'Craggs, who're you fucking looking at?'

'No-one.'

'No-one, Bob!' He demands

'No-one Bob,' I screech before I get knuckled.

'Who's got a fag?'

'Here Bob,' Tris offers. He even lights it for him with his silver lighter. Bob doesn't thank him.

'What're you all doing?'

We stand silently for a moment because we don't know what we're doing.

Paul breaks our awkwardness, 'Ah we're just hanging around.'

'Yeah,' we all join in, not wanting to be out of the dialogue.

'What're you bovver boys now?' He mocks.

Uncomfortable silence. Who among us has the balls to say yes?

'Rob is,' Tris says, 'he's got his new Dr. Martens on.'

'Craggs you wanker, have you kicked anyone's head in yet?' Bob mocks.

'No, none of us have,' I argued, 'We haven't had any fights yet.'

'Well, if you're a gang, you've got to have a fight. Go up to Hillcrest and have a fight with them, you've got to get known. Ave you got a gang name?' He asks

We all look at each other.

'We haven't got a name yet!' someone says.

'Well you can't call yourselves 'The Chulsa,' coz we're The Chulsa.'

Someone suggests 'Chulsa Juniors.'

'Chulsa Juniors, what are you fucking nursery kids?' Bob laughs, 'next you'll be calling yourselves The Chulsa Bumboys.'

We all snigger.

'Don't laugh,' he says 'Actually, when you all grow up, one of you is probably gonna be a queer. I saw it on TV.'

It occurs to me that Bob might be more intelligent than I realised. He watches documentaries. I'm immediately worried by this statistic he's shared.

We all look at each other and make noises of disgust and I wonder if anyone of them think it might be me that's gonna be queer. I put on the toughest look I can muster.

Bob's walking off, taunting with, 'Well you better get out and have a fight instead of walking around like a bunch of bumboy wankers.'

We start thinking and discussing what our gang name should to be. But I'm distracted. At the back of my mind, I'm worried. When I grow up, will I be the bumboy queer? Will I be the one cursed with this affliction? And can my mates tell?

CHAPTER 33 — Chulsa Oak

It takes a few brainstorming sessions to come up with our gang name. We want the name 'Chulsa' in our name, as it identifies where we're from. We go through all the possibilities, Chulsa Bovver Boys? Nah too long. Chulsa Lads? Yeah, maybe but hang on, we've got girls in our gang. So, we settle on 'Chulsa Oak.' 'Oak' referring to the oak tree down the bottom of the estate where we hang around smoking cigarettes. Within a week, one of my gang members has spray painted 'Chulsa Oak' on my front door and on the wall by our French windows. To this day, I don't know who did it. I'd still like to find out.

We never had gang fights but we found plenty of trouble. The first time was at the Crystal Palace Sports Centre. It was during the summer holiday; we'd been lazily wandering around, hot and listless when we noticed a Pepsi Cola van in the distant car park. The back was open and there were a few boys running away from it with cartons of Pepsi clutched under their arms. Opportunities like this didn't fall out of the sky, so we ran straight over, lifted off a carton each and ran off as fast as we could.

Somebody called the police and within minutes, a police panda car was chasing us. We could have escaped and some did but me and David Bacon were in hearing distance of the policeman, so when he shouted for us to stop, we did as he told us rather than run off. We dropped our booty to the ground and waited in dread. But when he caught up to us, he asked for our names and addresses and told us off for climbing over fences and to not do it again. We nodded with our mouths wide open and then he got back in his car and drove off, leaving us with our booty. We picked up our cartons, caught up with our mates and headed home with enough soft drink to last a whole week.

About an hour later there was a knock on the door. When I answered it, who was standing there? That same policeman and he wasn't looking happy. After he had left us in the park, someone had informed him of what our real criminal acts were. And he had my address.

Imagine the scene; Mum in the kitchen, all cheery, 'Who's at the door Robert?'

Me, realising that my life is over, shouting out with the deepest sorrow, 'you'd better come here Mum, I'm in trouble.'

'Eh.' as she appears at the kitchen doorway with the potato masher in her hand, now with a look of mounting fear as she sees me standing at the front door with a policeman.

I was in serious trouble and under pressure I caved and ratted on most of my mates. We received a caution from the police which meant going down to the police station and getting a serious telling off from a very bored policeman.

That wasn't enough to curb our waywardness. If there was trouble, we'd find it. Like the day we were walking up Crystal Palace Park Road and Terry yelled out that he'd seen a bloke flashing out of a window.

It was an empty derelict house that backed onto the park. Many of the houses on that road were derelict, all waiting for an injection of money and design ideas from a property developer.

We weren't scared, we were a gang! We would get that sick pervert and teach him a lesson. 'Let's get him,' said Grant.

'Yeah,' we all joined in.

We grabbed sticks and walked around to the back of the

house to find an entrance. It was a grey day, late afternoon; the garden overgrown with weeds, disquieting in contrast to the main road around the front with the secure noise of traffic. Untended shrubs and wild weeds suggested we were taking the first step into disregard, away from order. The back door was open but there was a huge ditch in front which dropped to the basement below. We each jumped over it and huddled by the door threshold, waiting to see who would lead the way into the house.

'You go Terry,' hissed Lakesie, 'You saw him, you know what he looks like.'

Terry, to my surprise, accepted the challenge and edged forward one slow step at a time with several of us pressed up behind him.

At first, I could see the back of Terrie's brown hair but as we crept further in, he disappeared, swallowed up by the darkness. I was terrified but we had started something we couldn't stop. The giggling and hoarse whispers disappeared and the tension and the atmosphere tightened up; we were a bunch of mousetraps ready to snap at any moment.

Terry turns a corner in the in the pitch-black silent corridor when the snap comes. 'ARRGGHHH!' I feel the instant realisation of danger as a weight of bodies turn against me scrambling in panic and fear. I twist around; all I can think of is getting out of that house. As I rush and push, I trip over Dave Bacon. It's blind mayhem and I'm trying to get onto my feet before the paedophile monster comes and takes me away to his dungeon bedroom but every time I get halfway up, someone knocks me back down in their panic to get away. I'll be left behind, I know it. Death will have me here, in this cold dark place. Every time I'm knocked down

I'm pushed closer to the ditch. If I fall down there, I'll be trapped. I'm doing everything I can to ensure I'm not knocked down into it.

Then it's all over, everyone's out except me and I'm kneeling right over the ditch waiting for that dirty pervert to come and get me, it's written in the stars, it was meant to be and I know it, I feel it.

Feeling weak with fear I'm not sure I can jump over the ditch. I need running space. I have to run back into the dark house where death awaits but I need a good run up to clear the ditch. I run into the darkness, expecting the hand to reach out and get me. But I'm lucky, the grinning dark doesn't take me this time and I leap over the ditch and away from darkness and into light and catch up to my gang who had left me behind to have my life buggered out of me.

As soon as we re-assemble we are overjoyed. It's like we've been reborn. We've been to hell and back. Then Terry sees the very man walking down the road, the one who had been flashing himself. Out in the open we're very brave once again and chase down the road after him, he will not get away. Not this time. As we bear up to him he turns to face us. He's surprisingly well dressed, smart casual, like a left-wing schoolteacher and he seems confident. He says nothing but his expression is one of, 'Can I help you?'

Now we've caught up to him I realise we don't have a plan. After a few seconds awkward silence one of us asks 'we're looking for the man who came out of that house up there, he was flashing himself, have you seen him?'

'Oh yes,' he says, 'I saw a man come out of that house, he went that way,' he points over to the park.

We don't know what's next, we are stuck, all we can say

is 'Thanks mate' and then we let him go and we make a big show of running towards the park in pursuit of the flasher.

None of us admits we had the guy and let him get away; that we had him in in our hands and didn't know what to do. How can we admit that he played us like a bunch of lambs?

CHAPTER 34 — Dare

There's a rumour that Hillcrest Estate wants to fight us. We go up there armed with milk bottles stuffed down our shirts; they were glass back in those days. I try to act tough but I'm scared, not only of getting badly hurt but also of getting into trouble by the police for carrying an offensive weapon. Nothing happens, a few police cars drive around and there's excitement in the air but Hillcrest doesn't show. I'm relieved.

On another evening, we walked down Ormanton Road by the bombsites. We stumbled on a gang of lads playing in the bombsite and had a small bonfire burning.

'Oy, you're not allowed in there.' Lakesie shouted

We all joined in with affirmative murmurs and there was the usual sizing up that happens when two tribes meet but before long, we were playing dare games with each other running over the bonfire along a plank of wood. We bonded and became mates. The Oak, as Chulsa Oak was also known, was about to grow.

The next time we nearly got into a big fight, it was my fault. We were down The Crypt and I was feeling great in my red and white-checked Ben Sherman shirt and tank top which I'd bought that day from Sherrick's. I had that feeling of hubris, a prideful excessive arrogance and it was about to get me into big trouble.

One of the kids at the club, like me, was mixed race, though back then we were called half-caste. He always had this tough snarl on his face. Well, I'd had enough of him. So I snatched his cigarette off him. I was always trying to earn brownie points like this.

Off I went, eager to show off my booty (one half of a

cigarette) to Paul Winston and Tris Miles, 'I just snatched a fag off some geezer.' I said, blowing smoke rings up into the air. Paul and Tris had slight smiles on their faces and motioned that someone was standing behind me. I turned around to see a tall bloke towering over me. He looked like Jaws out of the Bond movie, tall and ugly. He stared at me not saying a word. I gave him a stupid smile which he didn't return and I tried to work out what he wanted. The kid who I'd taken the ciggie from stood next to him and I realised he wanted his ciggie back. I held it in the air and then passed it to the big guy. He took it from me and then held it in the air and let it fall to the ground. Then he slowly and deliberately trod and twisted it into the ground with his shoe, all the time not once taking his cool eyes off me. Then he turned around and walked away.

I turned to Tris and Paul, shocked and humiliated but also relieved that he hadn't belted me but then Tris mouthed, 'Oh fucking hell, that's Maurice Trigg!'

Maurice Trigg? I knew that name, I'd heard all about him. I felt the fun of the whole evening draining down my legs, leaving me cold and joyless. As I stood there sinking, Tris added extra weight, 'You're in deep shit Craggsie, he's gonna fucking get you.'

A gulf emerged between me and my mates. I could see them standing in front of me. They may as well have been a million miles away. I was utterly on my own. How could it be that while standing on the same spot, they seemed to be basking in heaven while I baked in hell?

When the club finished, I was quaking, thinking him to be waiting outside for me but he was gone. Never mind, already the rumours started. Trigg was coming back to get me next week and bringing his gang with him.

Moving to Chulsa

What was I going to do? I could always stay at home but then everyone would call me a coward. Before I could worry any more, it emerged that because Trigg was bringing his gang to get me, another gang was coming along to help my gang. Before I knew it, I was an unknown pawn in an increasingly growing drama.

The next week came and something superb happened. My voice broke. Overnight, I suddenly sounded like Marlon Brando in 'The Godfather' and in that dark autumn evening sitting outside The Crypt waiting for Trigg, I was a new creation.

All these tough bovver boys standing around waiting for the fight, not one of them knew that the whole ruckus resulted from my actions. Trigg must have gotten wind of the situation and rode past the Crypt, with his mates, on the bus, no doubt checking the situation.

What he would have seen were scores of youths with chains, bottles, sticks and shining Dr. Martens, all hanging around and sitting on walls outside the church.

I never saw Trigg ever again though he sent a guy I knew, called Paul Brigdon, to the Crypt to get me the following week. He showed up with half a dozen lads but the club manager must have had a sixth sense and wouldn't let him in. Brigdon tried to coax me out, 'Come out here Rob, I want to talk to you.'

To my surprise, Bob Davisdon, the blond Neanderthal, who often delighted in roughing me up, came to the door and growled, 'If you've got trouble with Craggs, you've got trouble with me.'

Bob Davidson! He could be hard to digest, all rev but no thought, all battery but no steering wheel but in the blink of an eye, he blew my troubles away.

If we weren't getting into trouble with the police or other gangs or the neighbourhood, we'd still push everything to the limit. It was all about dare.

We played 'chicken' with a knife. Standing a few metres away from each other, the first one would throw the knife into the grass nearby the opponent's leg. Remaining standing where he was, the opponent would put one foot over the spot where the knife sank and if successful, he'd then sink the knife somewhere, near his opponent's leg.

This got boring, so we tried standing further away from one another, up to 50 metres and lobbing darts at each other. If you moved a muscle, you became chicken. Sometimes I became chicken, sometimes I got a dart stuck in my leg.

Next came bows and arrows. At first crudely made but Tim Belton, the quietest and thoughtful one of us, honed his skills. We all copied, cutting out pieces of playing cards for the arrow flight and soft lead to add weight to the sharp tip. Divided into two teams, hunting each other, flying arrows at each other all around the estate, hiding behind walls, it was great fun, exciting; it didn't last long. Tim shot Tris in the corner of his eye; he was lucky he didn't lose it. After that, led by Tim, we each sacrificially destroyed our bows and arrows in honour of safety.

We are opportunistic and discover fun anywhere and everywhere. There's a high wall; left over from a derelict house. A group of saplings is growing up next to it. We discover that if we climb onto the wall and jump off, grabbing the top of the saplings as we do, they bend over and we come flying down to the ground but at a safe speed. Some eventually snap and we crash down.

That doesn't stop us and we carry on for hours until eventually there's not one sapling left. I nearly embed myself on a jagged broken sapling when mine snaps. I miss the jagged splintered spear of the trunk by centimetres. It seems we exhaust everything except ourselves in our thirst for life.

CHAPTER 35 — Cwabby in the Cupboard

At about age 14 I'm the first of my mates to get a tattoo. Paul has come along with me on the 122 bus. All the way to Woolwich.

Big tough guys sat around in the parlour showing off muscles; no room for kids. But I'd come a long way; no backing out. The tattooist should have told me to get lost as I was too young to get a tattoo. Instead, he told me to sit down while he finished his work of art on some toughie. Meanwhile, me and Paul looked at the options on the walls; women laying back into champagne glasses, swallows, Popeye, dice, Rizla packs.

When my turn came, I asked him, 'What can I have for a pound?' He pointed to a section on the wall; I settled on skull and crossbones with a dagger going through its head. I expected it to be hand drawn but he pulled out a transfer, placed on the inside of my arm and traced it with his electric ink needle. Paul sat close by to watch for tears. It did hurt but no tears for Paul.

A few months later I visited another tattooist in Croydon. This time, Tris Miles and Simon Lake also came along. I wanted, a dove by the base of each thumb. On this occasion the tattoo artist, a big fella who looked like he could easily hurt people, turned out to be a caring bloke. His voice was soft for a big guy and he said I was too young and he wouldn't be able to tattoo me. At the time I felt embarrassed and Lakesie made fun of me all the way home on the bus. But if I met that tattoo artist today, I think I'd kiss him.

Talking about kissing, we had become interested in girls. Around that time a few girls older than us had taken us into their little circle for a short season. Rather than practice stuff with boys their own age, they chose us instead; we were safer and easier to control. One of them, Rita Donovan, was gorgeous, with red hair cut like Rod Stewart's.

I remember her singing Maggie May, 'Wake up Maggie I think I've got somethin' to say to you....'

She and a few of her mates played 'Dare' with me, Paul, Tris and a few others. It meant kissing too.

I know me and the lads loved it and Rita even told me I was a good kisser. But they were just trying out their skills on us; they soon left us for older boys.

I began to become bolder and realised that taking a day off school now and then was easy. I'd rather catch sticklebacks, play in the park and drink coffee and eat toast at mates' houses but a day off school needed a letter from the parent saying why the child was away. This could be the difficult bit. Sometimes a teacher could be fobbed off but Mrs Frost would not leave it. Every day, she'd press me for a letter from my mum about my school absence.

I tried to get Paul Newton to write it for me; he had lovely handwriting but even though he'd gotten me out of trouble before, he wouldn't do it again, even with threats of violence. I had to write it myself. It took many attempts trying to copy Mum's writing style; lots of crumpled paper ended up in the bin. I eventually presented my offering. Mrs Frost didn't seem convinced but she'd had enough and accepted the note and let the matter go.

That evening though, Mum wasn't impressed when she found all my forgery attempts in the kitchen bin. I didn't cover my tracks.

Poor Mrs Frost; I gave her a difficult time, she once told

me I was the worst boy in her class. I knew I wasn't a dedicated student but there were far worse lads in our class than me and I had nothing to do with Melvyn shooting her in the face with a paper pellet. In fact, I didn't even know anything about it until her shriek pierced the classroom, 'Who did that?'

I'd been sitting there, head down writing out the answers. I had no idea that Mel, who was sitting right behind me, had his paper pellet aimed at the back of my head, getting ready to send me some ripping pain. He had no idea that as he let that pellet go, I'd bend my head forward in studious pursuit right at that moment. He also had no idea that the pellet would whiz through the air at lightning speed and give Mrs Frost a big stinger on the side of her cheek.

I heard her yell and looked up to see her holding her red cheek with her hand and looking furious. How exciting. I turned around to see Mel sitting in the seat behind me, his face full of fear and as red as a beetroot. He slowly raised his hand, trying to put on a nice smile for her. Fantastic.

But he got off lightly. I wouldn't have. It probably didn't help that Mrs Frost had moved to an apartment near Chulsa and our gang made a nuisance of ourselves. Once she came out and told us all off and probably wondered if she'd chosen the wrong address. Also, there was the time she and my mum ended up in the headmaster's office with her getting a talking to on my behalf. Truanting had become a habit but the police had caught me and they hauled me into Headmaster Kingsman's, office. There was a lot of questioning and when I said I didn't like the teachers it wasn't long before Mrs Frost's name came up.

Truanting got me into a lot of trouble but for a short time it also made me locally famous.

Moving to Chulsa

Me and Ray Spearman had skipped an afternoon from school and were up at his house. He lived on a housing estate on Hawthorn Grove off Maple Road.

We sat around drinking coffee and eating toast in his bedroom. We always used to enjoy winding one another up, so when I stood by his window and saw a lady pushing the garden gate open and walking up the path. I guessed it was his mum. He thought I was lying.

'Just come to the window and look.' He did. I was about to gloat but he took off without a word. He flew out of that bedroom without a word, down the stairs and out the back door and gone as his mum's key clicked into the lock. In those split seconds I only made it to the top of the stairs, then seeing her reflection downstairs through the mottled windowpane of the door I ran to the back window. Ray was half-way up the garden path. He looked back and even had the cheek to wave goodbye.

I ran on tiptoes to Ray's bedroom with his dog following me around. 'Go downstairs Skip.' He wagged his tail. I was still looking for a place to hide as Mrs Spearman entered the house.

I was desperate. How was she going to react to a strange boy in her house? 'Hello Mrs Spearman, please don't be alarmed, I'm not a burglar, I'm just truanting in your house, Ray's gone for a walk.'

I was terrified and had to hide somewhere. I climbed into Ray's wardrobe, pulled the door closed and sat there wondering how long I'd have to sit and how the hell I would get out of the house. It didn't help that Skip kept coming upstairs scratching on the door. I opened the door a fraction to see him sitting there wagging his tail. 'Go away Skip!'

After a while, it all seemed silent and I wondered if Mrs Spearman had gone out shopping, so I got out of the cupboard and crept down the stairs. Skip heard me and came to the bottom of the stairway and stood there wagging his tail looking up at me. Thank goodness he wasn't a barker. I heard a scraping sound. I crept down a few more steps, looked over the banister and saw Mrs Spearman in the kitchen peeling potatoes. If she turned her head around, she'd have seen me and freaked.

I crept back up the stairs and as I did so, Skip started whining. I crept quietly along and got back into my wardrobe with Skip behind me. Then Mrs Spearman came up the stairs ordered Skip out of Ray's bedroom and I sensed her standing in the room for a minute. I tried to control my breathing, I felt I wanted to burst into tears and I started praying to God that I'd be a good boy from now on if he'd get me out of this mess. To my relief, she shut the door and went downstairs.

After about an hour Ray must have come home, I could hear his mum arguing. Then the fearful treading of stairs and the opening of the bedroom door as someone entered, then my worst fear, as the cupboard door opened. I crouched down like a poor beggar on the ground looking up for mercy with tears rolling down my eyes but whose face should I see but fucking Ray Spearman? Boy was I glad to see him. His mum knew he'd been truanting because he'd left the back door open but Ray's motto was 'deny everything.' Anyway, she'd gone out to the shops. Time for me to leave.

The story became well known for a while, especially at school and my mate Patrick Mint even wrote a song about it, 'Cwabby in the Cupboard,' to the tune and in the style of the recently released 'Big Seven' by that reggae artist,

Judge Dread.

Chorus - Hey hey diddle dumb day, Cwabby hiding in the cupboard

Hey hey diddle dumb day, Cwabby in the cupboard

Vs 1 - Cwabby and Ray had a good idea, to not bother going to school

They went to Raymond's house instead, coz they thought they were cool

Chorus

Vs 2 - They sat around drinking coffee and tea, they sat around eating toast

But then Cwabby saw Ray's mother, walking up the road

Chorus

Vs 3 - Ray was fast and he ran out the house, he left poor Cwabby behind

Cwabby had to be very quick, to find a place to hide

Chorus

Vs 4 - There was only one place he could hide, in the cupboard in Ray's bedroom

He sat there all the afternoon; hoping Ray would come home soon

Chorus

Vs 5 - What would Mrs Spearman say to him, if she caught him in the cupboard?

She'd think he was a burglar; she might stab him with a sword

Chorus

Vs 6 - Ray came home pretending that he'd been to school

His mother said to him, do you think I am a fool?

Chorus

Vs 7 - Then she went out to the shops, so Ray went to look for Cwabby

And he found him in the cupboard, on his knees and sobbing

Chorus

What a character Patrick was. He had a shock of curly blond hair as curly as mine and he looked like an angel, the politest rascal I knew. He came from an Irish family, his dad soft by nature and his mum always lovely but she apparently used to lay into Patrick heavily.

One day I was at Patrick's house and I knew his mum had been battling with cancer, I asked Patrick where she was?

'She died.'

This was serious. We were supposed to be very solemn. I felt a mad desire to laugh. I tried to hold it down but that made it worse. A huge bubble of mad laughter erupted from me. Patrick too. We sat there laughing our heads off at this news of his mother's death. Her death wasn't funny but it was bizarre. We couldn't cope with such a catastrophe. We laughed with raw passion, rolling on Patrick's bed but I felt the guilt. After that, we went out to play.

I never told Patrick how sorry I was for him to be losing his mother. The pain must have been insurmountable.

I didn't know it then but she had schizophrenia. I believe Patrick had mixed feelings about her death. Patrick developed it too. I remember Badger telling me how Patrick ran out from a pub one day. He ran out and found himself a quiet place and sat there trembling. Badger came after him. 'What's up, mate?' Patrick was crying, everyone was looking at him. He couldn't take it any longer. It didn't help when he got himself a job as a cook in a pub, miles away from home working split shifts with a four-hour break in the middle of the day. He fell into the habit of drinking during that break. The alcohol and the medication, a cruel mix. That poor boy became scary to be around.

He was once one of my best friends and I can't do anything to help him. I still think of him and the pain he suffered and what that illness did to his life.

CHAPTER 36 — Perverts

I'm a solid part of my gang but I've also started knocking around with Badger; he lives on Crystal Palace Park Road, just down the road from where I used to live. He'd always been a distant familiar figure; we'd had a run-in once in my earlier childhood. My friends and I had been playing over at Crystal Palace Park. The Coates' house, like ours, backed onto the park.

We would often climb from our garden over the fenced-off area between the park and our gardens — we named our bit 'Clay Island.' We discovered it, we named and claimed it. From Clay Island, we'd spill into the park, roaming around the sports centre, exploring the old palace ruins, rummaging in the pond and wandering around the old maze.

At one time we thought ourselves to be park keepers. In those days there were actual park keepers, employed by the councils. They wore rich brown jackets and trousers with a brown Trilby hat. They looked like gentlemen out strolling, only they'd stab up bits of rubbish with their long poker stick and they'd chase us away from forbidden areas like the ski slopes which we'd slide down on estate agents 'for sale' signs.

We became friends with one of them and we were soon making our own park keeper badges. One day we saw a man hiding in the bushes doing dirty stuff with his willy. As 'park keepers' we saw it as our duty to observe but he took off when he realised he had a big audience.

A few days later, as me and John Mitchell were going through the top entrance to the park, I saw this same man heading into the toilet. I had my park keeper badge on and I told John about my suspicions. 'Stay here John.' I said.

'I'll follow him into the toilets and see what he does.' I followed him into the toilet and stood a few urinals away from him, pretending to go to the toilet as I kept my eye on him. To my disgust, he was pulling on his thing like it was a piece of long rubber and then he turned around and gave me a sick smile and walked towards me, all the time performing his long rubber pulling motion. I stood there paralysed with fear thinking I was about to be kidnapped and would never be seen again. I screamed my head off.

He took off and a young couple nearby came rushing in to see what was going on. They called the police from a blue police box across the road from the park entrance. Within twenty minutes I was in a police car driving around the park looking for the dirty man but he'd gotten away.

I consider myself lucky. I had a few encounters throughout my years but nothing terrible ever happened.

My first dirty encounter happened when I was about four. I was up north at my grandparents, staying there for a few weeks. I loved it up there, I loved the Geordie accent and everyone was so friendly and fish and chips came with loads of batter scratchings. Faces would come and go, neighbours dropping by, all friends, all special.

Wheelchair Des seemed to know our family well and so he was ok by me. The front of his dark greasy hair had that fifties quiff which dropped into long unkempt hair. He wore a black leather jacket and thin dark-rimmed glasses. He was at our house once and everyone was talking and happy and friendly. Sweets and chewing gum were offered around and it looked like I was taking him out for a walk in his wheelchair. All smiles, up the garden path, out the gate, Grandmother and Mum waving and smiling and Des full of cheer. Then to his house and more adults smiling, talking and lovely hot chips with salt and vinegar, then Des says we're off to the golf course and I'm pushing him up the hill next to the course and we stop by the garages.

He's the boss, he's the grown up, he's in charge and even though I know what he wants is wrong, there's no way out.

I'm not even sure where he wants me to put my hand but it's difficult getting to it; to where he wants it to be. I'm pushing my hand as hard as I can up his trouser leg to reach where he wants me to put it. I'm pretending to try hard. I can feel something, something fleshy and I don't like it; thankfully it's over after a few minutes. It's a sour end to the happy day, it doesn't fit with the smiles, the friendly waves and the chips and I don't want to go to his house again and I never want to be alone with him again.

I don't tell my mum or my grandparents; I don't know how and I'm sure they'd be angry and may not even believe me.

A few days later and I'm out playing with Jimmy Clifton. His hair spikes up by itself. His forehead is short and his eyebrow loomed over his eyes. Even when he smiles, his face is a scowl. He has incredible energy and drive, doesn't believe in God and he can punch hard. He says his dad doesn't believe in God either. To prove it, he screams out to his dad, who is talking to two ladies outside his garden gate, 'Daa diven you not believe in God?'

It's the wrong thing to shout out, 'You keep your little mouth shut,' his dad retorts, 'Or I'll bring you in the hooose reet noe and tan yer backside.'

The two ladies look shocked though I don't know whether it's from his retort or the fact he might be an unbeliever.

We slink off and when we got around the corner, I freeze. 'What's up.' asks Jim. I point up the road to a distant figure wheeling himself along in a wheelchair. He's seen us and seems to hover. I tell Jim, 'He's dirty, he made me touch his willie.'

Without a thought and without a moment's breath, Jim turns toward the distant figure and yells out as loud as he can, 'Gan on yer dirty foockin bassddad, get the fook away from here.'

How simple; problem over. I never have to deal with Dirty Wheelchair Des again.

Jim never mentioned it again and I reckon he forgot the incident within seconds. That boy was so in the present!

He had no idea how important that act was for me. He wasn't being heroic as such. It was like him to face any challenge win or lose. He always had a bone to pick and once dealt with, he'd look for another.

There were other instances, like when I was at Crystal Palace getting fish and chips and I saw a man walking around the streets wearing a long raincoat. He seemed to be shaking.

I followed him to see what he was up to, never mind that my fish and chips were getting cold. Then he walked into a shop doorway and turned around. His raincoat was open and I could see why and what he was shaking. I looked at him in disbelief and he winked at me. I screamed while he took off. He was probably a harmless person, really. However, the man outside the sweetshop who asked me if I wanted to be in the movies didn't seem so harmless. He was smartly dressed and polished and oh how I wanted to be in the movies. But I said no, backed away and went straight home.

The nearest I got to being hurt was when I had come home from school and was heading over to the park with my Tonka lorry. I used to tie the Beano book on the top, then sit on it and go flying down the hill. One day an overly cheerful man stopped me. He seemed to know me and I felt I could trust him. He asked me if I knew him. I thought he looked familiar but I couldn't be sure.

'Where's your mum?'

'At work.'

He suggests we go up to my house and wait for her to come home. We go up to our house. Maybe it's good that Anne Stewart sees us going up but that doesn't deter him from doing a 'medical examination' on me.

I didn't want to do it but he's the boss and he's reassuring, 'It won't take long.' He smiles.

I'm perched on his lap, like a ventriloquist's doll and he's very interested in my backside but only with his fingers. Goodness, I was so lucky. If Anne hadn't seen us, would he have stayed longer and been bolder?

Now I'm getting fifteen minutes of fame. The police have become involved and have alerted my school about the stranger danger. They announced the incident during assembly. Some kids have found out I'm the one. I tell them how the fella had pulled my pants down and had stuck his finger up my bum. They give looks of astonishment as if I'd achieved something fantastic.

CHAPTER 37 — World Cup

It's the second year of high school and Badger has joined with the influx of newbies fresh from the junior schools. Every time we bump into each other, he greets me with, 'Watch'ya Rob, how's your nob.' I find this attempt at friendliness tiresome but despite his immaturity, we're becoming good buddies. Honestly, he's sometimes far more mature than me and more empathetic too.

I must admit his sister was a strong motivation. She was beautiful with fine blonde hair, high flat cheekbones and lovely blue eyes. Smitten as I was, I didn't interest her, though I was too thick skinned to see that. Though I saw her as my discovery, my best mate Tris was the one who'd win her love.

It was 1970 when Badger and I started hanging around together. I remember because the 1970 World Cup Football in Mexico had started.

Castrol petrol stations had put on an incentive offer of 'English football squad' display boards with silver coins inserted into the cut-out circles on the board. Each silver coin, which they handed out with each visit to the petrol station, had an engraving of an English squad team soccer player on it. The aim was to be the owner of a filled display board.

Badger's dad drove a Castrol truck and was always filling his tank. He had given Badger a whole completed board with all the players in no time at all and Badger asked his dad if he could get one for me because I didn't have a dad. I couldn't understand it but Badger felt sorry for me. I didn't feel sorry but I had no objectivity and I doubt my ego would have wanted inward inquiry.

It was June when the world cup began and England was in the same group as Brazil. In the first round, we beat Romania 1-0 but Brazil beat the Czechs 4-1. Brazil then beat us 1-0 but so far we had 4 points which was respectful enough, even though Brazil and West Germany had 6 points each. But we made it through to the Quarterfinals and met West Germany.

It was hot in Mexico and the European soccer players had to take salt tablets because the excessive sweating leached out their body salts; today they'd be drinking electrolytes! It was hot at home too, every house on the estate that night of the England vs West Germany match had their windows open. Walking along the road outside you could hear the whole game and the screaming to go with it. Every family on our estate was connected to one another that night through the heat and excitement, even through the air. We were all one mass.

Mullery scored the first goal for England after 30 minutes to shouts and screams of delight filling the hot evening air. Twenty minutes later Wright scored another which put us 2-0 in the lead. This was it, English supremacy over the Germans. It was like winning the war again. But after 20 minutes, Beckenbaur scored a goal for Germany. We were still one goal up though, so we now had to play a more defensive game but 8 minutes before the final whistle, Seeler scored the equaliser for Germany.

Poor England, the Germans knew how to fight back even when under pressure. It looked like the game would be a draw which meant it would go to extra time. Both teams put on a hell of a fight to score a goal. Every time the Germans cracked hard at the English defence I had my hands in my mouth screaming at the possibility of a Deutsche victory. And every time the English got near the

German goal my heart rose, only to be deflated as the opportunity vaporised against the well organised German wall of defence.

It was a draw, so the match went to extra time, 15 minutes each way. The first half was rather uneventful as the teams sized each other up to see what tactics they'd use but in the second half Mueller scored within three minutes and that's how the game ended, with a German victory over England 3-2. England was out and I was deflated with misery. But at least the Italians knocked the Germans out 4-3 the following week.

Brazil win the cup with a 4-1 victory over Italy. They play incredible soccer and every person in the world roots for Pele, the top Brazilian player in the world. I love my Castrol World Soccer Coin Collection but it will get ripped and shredded through the wild winds of teenage years. I just don't look after things. In 40-years' time I'll buy a second-hand one off eBay for Badger's dad as a 'thank you.'

CHAPTER 38 — Windfall and Change

I'm bonded to my mates at Chulsa Oak but my new mate Badger who isn't a part of the gang is fast becoming a good mate of mine and I'm trying to bring these two sides of my social life together but it doesn't work at first. Badger isn't an 'estate' type of kid.

We'd all been experimenting with alcohol. At least once a week, we'd go down to the off license with our pocket money, buy ourselves a big bottle of cider and hide in the bushes behind Sydenham Girls High School. We'd sit under damp branches for half an hour pouring golden nectar down our throats before going out to play.

One afternoon after school, Simon Lake, Lakesie and I filled a milk bottle from his parent's drink cabinet. Hoping his parents wouldn't notice we pinched from each bottle: Tia Maria, Cointreau, Vodka, Whisky, Martini, Gin, Rum, Bacardi. Then off we walked down the road sharing swigs from our crazy cocktail. We got smashed in no time and before I knew it, I was sitting on the sofa at home trying to untie my shoelaces, my fingers getting into a bigger knot than my laces. I don't know where Lakesie had gone. My mother was looking at me asking questions about my state while I sat there smiling, still trying to untie my laces. Debbie intrigued sat nearby staring at me. I continued trying to untie my laces. Such a simple task. I could do it if…

If what?

What?

What is 'what?'

What is?

What is 'is?'

All my thoughts lined up before a blank wall and disintegrated into nothing. Thought left me. Nothing but blank; and shoelaces. And Mum looking at me waiting for an answer. An answer to what? And Debbie. I started to smile but tears came out; easily too. I enjoyed it! Mum burst out laughing.

One Sunday afternoon Tris had been drinking and we went up to Badger's with Paul Winston. Badger's sister, Laura, came out to say 'Hi.' Then right out of the blue Tris told her he loved her boobs and could he hold them? With that, he reached out and grabbed them. We howled with laughter as we pulled him back but she seemed to like the attention. She found the whole episode hilarious and so did I but I wished it was me grabbing her boobs. I noted that alcohol helps create the bridge.

The following weekend, Badger's mum and dad were going out for the evening. Tris and I were invited up for the evening.

We were listening to Deep Purple and Laura asked me if I wanted another drink. Feeling brave thanks to the cider, I stood up, took her into my arms and said, 'no, I want you' and then kissed her. What nirvana!

The kiss felt like forever but time seemed to be stretching and contracting. I became aware of both Tris and Badger complaining I should give Tris a go. I wish I'd told them to screw themselves but under pressure, I backed off and let Tris have a go. And that was my downfall. Tris and I kept taking her off each other like she was a rag doll. It reminded me of Tom and Jerry trying to outwit each other.

But the realisation set in. Laura wanted Tris. That was a truth I had to learn to accept. Here's another truth. Tris was a craftier player than me. The bastard locked himself in the bathroom with Laura, keeping me at a distance. Anyway, over the next few days Tris and Laura became an item.

From that point on, both Tris and I pulled away from the Chulsa gang and Badger, me, Tris and Laura spent all our time up at their house on Crystal Palace Park Road.

Life at Badger's place was fantastic; he had a huge garden and his dad picked up an old run-down motorcycle and Badger spent hours, days and weeks, trying to fix it up to get it running so we could ride it around the garden. It was the healthiest part of our teen hood; we had a lot of good, real clean fun, out in the garden, swinging on the tyre and riding around a big track on the motorbike, shooting each other in the backside with the air rifle.

The Coates' also had a small shed; it was in good condition but needed a good cleanout. We washed it down put a couple of beds and chairs in it and a small camping stove and soon we were enjoying our own little pad. We even did sleepovers at the weekends. Then, to add to our near perfect paradise, we were blessed with a huge windfall.

Every year at Crystal Palace Park, there was a rock concert just over the fence from Badger's back garden. Many stars played there including David Bowie, Lou Reed and Bob Marley. We always sneaked in without paying.

Well Badger and I had bunked over late in the afternoon and it became dark and heavy and soon the rain came down until it was coming down in sheets, cleaning the area of all people. The band packed up and all the hawkers and the bars, take-way cafés and stalls became deserted, leaving behind the burgers still warm on the griddles.

We stood there on the grass under the pouring rain, getting soaked, looking around. All we saw was opportunity. The first realisation was that we could help ourselves to burgers and cokes. We hopped over counters and stood under the gazebos watching people clear out of the park as we enjoyed our treats.

After a few burgers, we took a few supplies home to our shed; big commercial tins of burgers, cartons of cokes, stacks of paper plates, sets of plastic cutlery, stacks of plastic cups we thought would come in handy for pouring our drinks into but later discovered each cup to have a measure of dried milk, sugar and chocolate powder. What a bonus! Just add water!

Badger and I carried off as much as we could and lobbed it over the fence to the back of his garden and packed it into the shed. Then I said, 'goodnight' and headed home.

When I came back the next morning, Badger had a huge surprise for me. He and Tris had met up after I had gone home and together, they worked through half the night going around all the stalls and getting all the drinks, buns and burgers they could carry.

We had huge plastic bags of dried onions and gallons of tomato sauce to go with our endless supply of burgers. We had enough supplies to last the whole summer. Our shed looked like a warehouse. We even each took supplies to each of our homes and lived off burgers for months. Mum wanted to know where I'd gotten all this stuff. I think I told her that Badger's dad got it off the back of a lorry. She thought it best to not ask too many questions.

Well, our summer of good fortune didn't last. I remember reading an anthropological book on apes and there was an account of these apes splitting into two groups and one group decided after a while to hunt down the group that split away and kill them. The narrator said they regarded the split-off group as competition. It made me think of 'Lord Of The Flies' and tribalism.

There was no sun in the sky, the light cool. Dull but mild. When I think back to that late afternoon in the park with Tris and Badger and seeing our old gang, Chulsa Oak approaching us, they looked like a tribal hunting party. They came in force, led by Paul Winston, my old mate. But in this setting, he was more nemesis than mate. There was tension there between us but it was Lakesie who had an apparent grudge with Badger and he wanted to fight him.

What a farce! Lakesie wasn't a fighter, he had never been the aggressive type and he and Badger had always been the best of mates in the past, anyway Badger didn't want to fight. I tried to talk Lakesie out of it but he seemed determined, no doubt primed up by Chulsa Oak. We tried to encourage Badger to fight, we knew he had a good chance of beating Lakesie but Badger refused.

Badger wasn't a coward, less so than me but he didn't want to face up to Lakesie. I offered to stand in for him but everyone rejected the idea.

So, Lakesie started on Badger and Badger wouldn't hit back and it got ugly, Lakesie kept slugging and Badger was in tears and wouldn't hit back. Lakesie just kept going at him until me and Tris stepped in and said 'Enough!'

The beating seemed to raise our group tension, so we all agreed to have a free-for-all fight. Badger seemed good for this, so me Tris, Badger, Paul, Lakesie, Grant, Tracer, Jeffries and Ripper, we all just flew at one another like wolves.

Moving to Chulsa

I had been looking forward to this; I was aching to fight Paul and ran straight at him. The feeling was mutual and he ran at me too and it was rough; the knees on my jeans ripped open on the tarmac and I had cuts all over my hands afterward. The fight seemed to ease the tension between us and we all hung out together for the rest of the afternoon as if nothing had happened.

From that day on, our innocent days up at Badger's changed. Chulsa Oak came to put an end to our little offshoot group and it worked; the two groups became one.

I'm fourteen and have lived on Chulsa for a few years. But today, on this beautiful mild autumn afternoon, the summer is over and the leaves are turning. My Chulsa identity is more solid than ever. My old gang Chulsa Oak has hunted me, Tris and Badger down and in a flash, they've amalgamated us back into the old gang.

I'm pissed off.

But I feel love.

Acknowledgements

I'd like to thank Wendy and Maureen for their support and encouragement and my editor Claudette whose careful eye did not let a jot wander.

And lastly Mum for supplying me and Deb with all her marvellous stories over many glasses of wine. She has always been our family storyteller and it's with fondness that I look back to those nights. :)

www.ingramcontent.com/pod-product-compliance
Lightning Source LLC
Chambersburg PA
CBHW070253010526
44107CB00056B/2444